Executive Editor: Bobbye Middendorf
Managing Editor: Jack Kiburz
Editorial Assistant: Jill Strubbe
Interior Design: Publishing Services, Inc.
Cover Design: Design Alliance, Inc.
Cover photography: Janet Koltick

© 1996 by Milton Gralla and Adriane G. Berg

Published by Dearborn Financial Publishing, Inc.®

Printed in the United States of America

96 97 98   10 9 8 7 6 5 4 3 2 1

Library of Congress Cataloging-in-Publication Data

Gralla, Milton.
    How good guys grow rich : proven strategies to achieve financial success and lifelong satisfaction / by Milton Gralla & Adriane G. Berg.
        p.   cm.
    Includes bibliographical references and index.
    ISBN 0-7931-1531-0 (cloth)
    1. Success in business. 2. Success. 3. Businessmen—Psychology.
I. Berg, Adriane G. (Adriane Gilda), 1948- . II. Title.
HF5386.G66   1995
650.1—dc20   95-37800
                                                                  CIP

Adriane G. Berg & Milton Grall

HOW GOOD GUYS GROW RICH

Proven Strategies To Achieve
Financial Success and Lifelong Satisfaction

Dearborn
Financial Publishing, Inc.

Dedications

From Milt

To Shirley . . .
. . . My helpmate, buddy, adviser, inspiration, partner!

From Adriane

To my Mother, Gertrude Berg . . .
. . . Who taught me the invincible power of goodness.

Acknowledgments

Many thanks to Ethyl Spivack and Danielle Lemma for their conscientious attention to our needs, and their valuable contributions in preparing this manuscript. They are true symbols of the Good Guy spirit.

M.G. and A.B.

Contents

Preface

Do Nice Guys Really Finish Last?

Nonsense!! Patient good guys achieve wealth by enriching others.

Why are so many of the business and professional men and women of the world running sprints, when the race to success and prosperity is a marathon?

Countless thousands possess skill, talent, education, energy, ambition, confidence . . . all the right tools needed to cash in on the wealth opportunities of a free economic system. Yet for every one who reaches the top, scores drop out at the start or in the middle, with dreams never realized, potential never fulfilled, fortunes never gathered.

In decades of watching this race as a business publisher, I became convinced that, with more patience and vision, talented thousands could have reached the top. But they failed to concentrate on daily and consistent "Good Guy" behavior in the marketplace. This simple philosophy, correctly applied, is the more certain trail to the top.

However, this conclusion did not come quickly. I grew up in a world impacted by Leo Durocher's famous remark that "Nice guys finish last." News media periodically reported the misbehavior of the rich as if it were their special privilege. Movies made heroes of Bad Guys like the conspirators in *How to Succeed in Business Without Really Trying* and *Other People's Money.*

Millions of have-nots judged the ultra-rich with suspicion, convinced that every path to wealth was littered with broken laws and discarded ethics. When a millionaire lawbreaker went to prison, the common belief was: "Everybody does it. He made only one mistake; he got caught."

On the other hand, I discovered—separated from the headlines and hardly ever exposed to the public eye—a multitude of happy, inventive, honorable and extremely prosperous achievers in many fields of endeavor. Their behavior ran opposite to common belief. They enriched employees, their communities, clients, suppliers, and the worlds of all they met. They pursued lives "on the give," while public propaganda focused on just a few millionaires "on the take."

Did the positive lives of these superachievers come from instinct, or intentional design? I'll never be sure. I do know that certain attitudes and practices, assembled and outlined in this book, were characteristic of most of them.

Our business universe, with its roster of multimillionaires, is characterized primarily by Nice Guys whose path to the top is marked by admiring colleagues, associates, employees, customers and clients whom they have enriched instead of exploited. They haven't seen the inside of a prison like the junk-bond king or the hotel queen. They haven't coped with grand juries or committees of unhappy creditors. They haven't slept in countless strange beds, or contended with annual IRS income tax auditors, like the few better-known "headline heroes" we read about.

The hunger for the fast buck eventually teaches a bitter lesson to greedy, first-time jobholders, excessively impatient new recipients of important professional degrees, experienced workers daring a first effort in their own enterprises, and executives casting ethics aside for an impatient climb up the ladder. But patient, consistent Good Guy business habits bring wealth.

That's what this book is all about.

First, it promises you that a career "on the give" is a more certain marathon to wealth, while impatient pursuit of wealth "on the take" is a short sprint to nowhere. Second, it gives you, in a series of practical chapters and true-life examples, a step-by-step road map right to the top.

When you have completed *How Good Guys Grow Rich,* you'll be ready to apply this philosophy to employees, colleagues, every new contact in the business world and scores of situations and people on the challenging landscape of free enterprise.

You have one business life to live. Live it as a Good Guy! Follow this trail! Win the marathon!

Milton Gralla

A Testimonial from Adriane, Who Has Been a Student of Milt's Good Guy Method

Does this sound like you?

- Lots of excellent qualifications, hardworking, better than most at what you do, but often running behind the competition . . .
- A real softie for the underdog, an advice giver, a helper, sometimes a patsy . . .
- Cringing at complaints, ready to blame yourself when things go wrong, never exactly at the right place at the right time . . .
- Susceptible to flattery, nonconfrontational, and apt to hide your light under a bushel . . .

If this describes you, then these are some of the traits I share with you as a Good Guy, and we have both sometimes seen ourselves and acted like a loser instead of a winner. Milt has seen numerous folks try to get ahead by being Bad Guys and failing. I have seen just the opposite: numerous Good Guys turning sure success into failure because they were timid, self-effacing or just plain scared of rejection.

Milt's Good Guy method works for both types—both those in danger of falling for the greed syndromes of the 1980s, and those in danger of fading away because they can't confront prospects, clients and customers.

The Good Guy methodology is a source of spiritual pleasure for me. I am never in a position of asking more than I give; I am always in control because I am on the give, never on the take; I am never rejected for anything or by anyone, because I am there to help others. Yet, the financial rewards keep rolling in. I am no longer uncertain of the amount to charge nor do I fear getting "stiffed." I am confident that people want my help and are willing to pay for it.

Moreover, my instincts have changed. I no longer choose to help individuals because I feel sorry for them. My work is too important and rewarding to jeopardize it. Because good people rely on me, I owe it to them to hire excellence, not charity cases. Also, I gravitate more to winners, because they can accept and use what I have to offer. The bottom line is that I am financially comfortable and have the dollars to contribute to charity. I think that's win-win.

Ultimately, this is a book not only about business, but also about human nature. It enables you to retain customers by treating them right; it helps you make sales by giving, not taking; and it helps you to grow your business by surrounding yourself with appreciated and appreciating staff. But, that's just the half of it!

Being a Good Guy relieves stress. It is very wearying to make and take hostile phone calls, receive and write nasty letters, scheme, plot and outflank the next guy. Best of all, being a Good Guy gives you lots of opportunities in your workday to enjoy life. Try it; you'll like it.

Adriane G. Berg

CHAPTER 1

◇

Start Enriching Others (and Yourself) Today

Use These 20 Most Useful Ways To Enrich Others . . . and You're on the "Good Guy" Road to Wealth!

This book is filled with practical ideas and suggested skills by which to pursue wealth via the patient daily enrichment of others. Some require detailed explanation and practice. Others can be understood, adapted and applied overnight.

As a start, we have assembled 20 basic guidelines to help any established or novice business person achieve the switch from self-interest to the service of others.

Some of these are mentioned only once, while others are extracts or previews of forthcoming chapters. The immediate application of most or all of these practices will produce a quick change in your personal satisfaction, reputation in the business community and ultimate career success.

1. Praise the Positive

Watch for and seize every opportunity to appreciate the positive behavior of employees, colleagues, partners, suppliers and any others in your business process.

1

Quickly praise anyone who does more than expected, handles a job well, achieves above-average results, shows growth or otherwise stands out. You'll achieve both loyalty and the likely result that the recipient of praise will now perform at that level forever.

Egoist executives secretly enjoy correcting the faults of others; it makes them feel superior. However, Good Guys get much more mileage by finding and supporting positive behavior. As a result, their positive training efforts find more acceptance.

2. Take Responsibility

Assume and accept responsibility ... even when you're hurting! The world rewards responsible leaders ... not those who try to duck by explaining what went wrong, or who was at fault.

Here's a true story from the early career of a (now) multi-millionaire entrepreneur:

"I had to call an important customer and admit that a vital delivery deadline would be missed. I felt embarrassed and defensive, and started explaining what happened. He interrupted me and said: 'Andy, I like you, and am giving you some important advice. The world doesn't care about explanations. If you deliver, no explanation is needed. If you fail, no explanation makes a difference.'

"I never forgot that incident and that simple but wonderful advice. My later wealth flowed from concentrating on serving the needs of others, so that explanations were unnecessary."

3. "Good Enough" Is NOT Good Enough!

Never be satisfied to be merely "good enough" at a job. Everything done better makes a difference to your clients, to your colleagues, and to your own self-discipline.

When Milt graduated with some distinction from junior high school over 50 years ago, the principal advised: "Milton, some day someone will hand you a broom and ask you to sweep the floor. Don't be insulted. Sweep that floor better than it's ever been swept before . . . not just for him, but for yourself!"

Then he wrote in Milt's graduation yearbook:

"In whatever you're doing, aim to excel,
For what is worth doing, is worth doing well!"

The system worked!

4. Invest in Others

Invest generously and consistently in the skills, growth and performance of your employees. On a scale of 1 to 100, the typical successful executive or entrepreneur usually performs on a near-perfect level of 90 to 95. On the same scale, the executive's employees range from 40 to 90. Let's make the average 65.

Out of habit or ego, most "90-up" executives give excessive time to improving their own work, gaining great satisfaction from even further *personal* results. But the more visionary Good Guy's priority focuses on the staff of "65s." He or she progresses and profits much more quickly by bringing a handful or a few dozen of them up to the level of "90"-performers.

Good Guys extend their know-how to others. They never stop training, encouraging, rewarding, supervising and teaching their armies—large or small—up the ladder to excellence! (See Chapter 3, "Selecting, Enriching and Empowering Your Good Guy Team.")

5. Play Straight

Never make a private or secret business decision that you would be embarrassed to have known by others. Greedy Guys with limited vision bend the truth to make a sale or solve a problem. They function at either end of payoffs, doctor up insurance claims, commit tax fraud (because "everybody does it"), and cast aside ethics any time greater profit looms.

Good Guys make life's business decisions with the knowledge that the world has keen vision and a sharp memory. Their individual destinies depend on how others see them, and whether others trust them.

Turn away from any "extra buck" or tempting gain whose price represents a compromise of your reputation! Sooner or later you'll be in the elite company of those whom the world trusts completely. You'll be a rich Good Guy!

6. Hire Right the First Time

Don't let any crisis force you to "hire in a hurry." Look for the employee who will serve well for the next 20 years . . . not the stop-gap who may hold the fort for the next 20 days.

Good Guys recognize that the "fast hire" often hurts their own long-term interests, fellow employees, and even the newly hired but unqualified employee!

Sins to avoid when hiring under time pressure:

- Failure to check references
- Excessive and unrealistic promises
- Failure to provide test period or escape hatch
- Too many job responsibilities too quickly

7. Put Priorities Before Pleasures

Immediacy is a nearly universal characteristic of the world's multimillionaires. Creative challenges or nonglamorous routines (mailing lists, expense reports, an accounting mess) deserve equally prompt attention. The decks are cleared today for tomorrow's storm or opportunity.

A world-known industrialist related this secret for picking future executives:

"In the process of orienting every new employee, I provide something to study, and make an appointment for a test a week later.

"Four days later, I call the applicant in and administer the test.

"Nine out of ten protest that they're not ready; the allotted week hasn't elapsed.

"The tenth one runs through the whole test with flying colors, having sensed instinctively that there was no reason to delay any important and useful achievement. This achiever with a super sense of immediacy almost always makes it up the ladder faster and higher."

8. Request Multiple Business Cards

Always ask for two or three business cards . . . never just one! Your business contact will be flattered, impressed and often curious: "Why do you want two or three cards?"

Your simple, truthful explanation:

"I want to retain one business card for my own use and reference. But there are others I know who may want to reach you—colleagues in my own firm, mutual friends, business associates who may not know about you, etc. I used to regret asking for only one card. Never again. Give me two cards, and our meeting will be twice as useful."

This book hasn't enough pages to relate the positive results of this simple practice!

9. Give Your Cards Long Life

Before giving your own business card (or two), write something on the back. It might be the date you met, the matters you discussed, or some future information or service you can provide. Be sure the wording makes an offer of help, not a request for business!

Most proffered business cards are thrown out quickly. Yours will survive as a seed of future success if it contains a message "on the give."

10. Don't Buy the Cheapest

Never buy or sell at the very, very, very lowest price. The ranks of the world's most prosperous and most highly regarded professionals include very few who value their products, services or time at rock-bottom price. You would not eat the cheapest food, wear the cheapest clothes, live in the cheapest residence or buy the cheapest car. The lowest price usually is based on skimpy quality, service or performance.

If you buy too cheaply, disappointment will follow soon. If you sell too cheaply, you confess you're devoid of other values.

Milt's favorite example is a seminar given some years ago by his brother and lifetime business partner, Larry Gralla. Larry was a relative newcomer to a convention of fellow publishers, many of them with second-generation or third-generation companies. But the achievements of Gralla Publications were known to one and all.

The theme of Larry's lecture: "Charge enough . . . and don't try to sell everybody!" Did his system work? A few years later, Larry negotiated the deal to sell their company for $73 million!

11. Relatives? Proceed with Caution

Leave an "escape hatch" whenever you employ or go to work for any family member. Family-related businesses often thrive, but Good Guys know they might not. When there's no prearranged escape hatch, families and enterprises are in great danger. (See Chapter 5 for more on this volatile topic.)

12. Listen

Make yourself a good listener. Some of the world's most brilliant, talented, energetic potential entrepreneurs become losers as a result of "running mouth disease." In the business world, it is more profitable, verbally, to receive than to transmit.

Particularly during the first contact with anyone in the business world, train yourself to ask questions, listen with sincere interest, write down what the Other Guy says, and withhold switching the invisible spotlight from the new contact to yourself. Your reward will be friendship, open doors, new clues to going "on the give."

Habitual "transmitters" quickly lose their audiences. Listeners become rich Good Guys.

13. Offer Home Mailings

Diplomatically offer some of your best clients and contacts the option of receiving your informative mail at their home addresses. This applies to newsletters, catalogs, periodic announcements. While most will decline, the few who accept will give your mail more attention in the privacy and convenience of their homes. You become a very Good Guy to those who accept this option.

14. Read and Learn

Take time to read everything pertinent to your business—association reports, business pages, trade magazines, newsletters, research, etc. Business and professional fields change rapidly. Information is vital insurance for profitable decision making.

Good Guys also find their careful, systematic reading has wealth-producing by-products:

- News and articles you can clip out, duplicate, and send to preferred clients
- Tidbits you can condense and insert in your periodic newsletters (See Chapter 8 on newsletters)
- Useful ideas and data you can circulate to your own employees
- New issues to discuss with your lawyer, banker, accountant, insurer, or other service professionals

15. Assist Those Out of Work

Reach out to temporarily unemployed job-seekers in your profession or industry. Offer information, leads, references, useful input. You're seen as a supportive Good Guy, and it's personally satisfying to encourage anyone under stress. Many of these friends will return to decision-making positions in your field, and you'll be remembered.

The next time you hear of anyone in your field who is temporarily "on the street," ask for a few resumes and keep them available for "networking."

16. Utilize New Skills Promptly

If you have acquired or studied a usable new skill or good idea, apply it promptly. Any new skill is likely to be forgotten or discarded unless used promptly.

A true confession from Milt: "It took me over five years to figure this out. Our annual three-day sales meetings were hailed by our sales staff as 'great . . . terrific,' etc. But we found most attendees going right back to old habits without using valuable new skills and ideas. Why? There were no supervisors, deadlines, or provisions to ensure immediate application of what the salespeople had learned. The results changed when we assigned prompt practice and use."

Good Guys never stop growing. If you learn it and like it . . . try it!

17. Be Motivated To Help

Scour your notes and memory each day for any opportunity to be a helper or information contributor to that day's contacts. Write a letter, send a news item, send a card, send an idea. Show how you helped or can help. Go "on the give" with speed and imagination! (See Chapter 6 on letter-writing.)

18. Enrich Community and Industry

Give time, service, money or other input to one or more causes in your community or industry. Ask nothing in return.

We live at a time and under circumstances that are the envy of the world. These are gifts to us from past generations of pioneers, visionaries and givers. Now it's your turn. Pay your dues joyfully. The world has its own balance scale and magic formula for noticing and rewarding your "giving" behavior. (See Chapter 16 on this topic.)

19. Ambition, Yes . . . Greed, No!

Differentiate between ambition and greed. Ambition is positive. It's essential en route to the top.

Greed is dangerous and usually comes in the disguise of a short-cut. It opens the door to embarrassment, scam, disrepute, evil business practice. See Rule 20.

20. Avoid Tempting Traps

Remember that "if it's too good to be true, it probably isn't." You can't double your money in six months risk-free; escape easily from a limited partnership whose promoters didn't deliver on rosy promises; enforce verbal commitments if it is determined that the fine print contained a disclaimer; get your money back from an off-price supplier who quickly disappeared; or otherwise get rich fast on the tempting menu of "sure things" invented daily by Bad Guys.

—————— ◇ ——————

APPLYING THE GOOD GUY METHOD TO SEE ASTONISHING RESULTS

How Adriane Used Her Genuine Interest in Others To Create a Million-Dollar Radio Show

Radio advertising, a field Adriane knows very well, is a great case for the Good Guy method. A top ad manager reported that financial sponsors re-buy only 30 percent of the time. That means that 70 percent of the sponsors are lost as long-term, repeat customers. Salespeople are left to sell to new prospects, a much harder task than reselling to old, loyal customers.

The reason for such turnover is clear. Sales are made without taking the time to build relationships, or to monitor the audience response to the client's product or service. As in many industries, the commission structure focuses on immediate numbers, the monthly gross sales. It doesn't recognize a steady, growing client base with low turnover as the powerhouse for the future that it will surely become.

We are living in a world that measures success by the minute.

In 1991, the programming at WABC Radio, where Adriane hosts a legal and financial advice show, changed to favor the very popular "hot talk" political format. Adriane either had to help the sales force make the show a rollicking financial success, or she was out. "Believe me, I'm no salesperson—not by training, not by temperament. I'm a Good Guy. I like to help, give advice. That's what I do."

It was at this time that Adriane and Milt were beginning to discuss the ideas for this book. Adriane began to realize that natural helpfulness is a plus, not a drawback.

Adriane notes: "I could have tried to 'hustle' clients, begged some friends in the industry to do me a favor by advertising, or hired a sales team to compete with the excellent WABC sales force; but all of that felt wrong. I just kept wondering, 'If professional sales people can't keep financial sponsors, how will I?' So I decided to find out. The next week I visited every sponsor— and I just listened: I took notes; I heard how they make their money, who they are, what they loved in life; I looked at their offices, their family pictures, the plaques on their walls.

"The next Sunday, I threw away the canned copy and, instead, I told my listeners about the sponsors. I individualized them, explained what they can do for their customers.

"I got personal, they got business, and I have a show that's been going strong with loyal sponsors ever since. I once heard a salesperson say: 'Adriane's show sells itself.' Don't you believe it! The sell may not be the traditional churn 'em and burn 'em, but it succeeds through the efforts of everyone involved working hard to bring quality financial services and luxury products to the public. The ultimate 'how to' tip—and the first rule of Good Guyism—is *Focus on the other guy*. You will be astonished by the rewards."

Although this revolutionary idea that "goodness equals reward" may seem a trendy '90s thing, Good Guy success is no accident or fad. Successful people everywhere employ direct, provable methods that you can start to use in the next hour which will demonstrate the Good Guy you are and make you a rich guy as well.

SILENT SURVEY #1

Go back and review the 20 basic guidelines of the Good Guy method, or "the gospel according to Milt." Ask yourself these questions:

- Do I already do this?
- Consistently?
- When was the last time?
- What was the beneficial result?
- Am I aware and conscious of my behavior in this category?
- For each of the 20, what can I do today to be closer to the Good Guy behavior pattern?

Let's take a look at numbers 18 and 19 to see how profoundly these seemingly simple tenets can change your business, even your life.

Number 18 suggests that you give service. In the spirit of the Silent Survey, do you? Not money, but time. If you don't, you are falling short of the example of successful Good/Rich Guys. If that's what you want to be, you must get out there and give help. Try reading to kids at the local library once a week, fundraise for your college, or give out child-abuse information at the local supermarket for an hour each week. Do whatever gets to your heart.

Giving creates a power base that can't be calculated and probably can't be explained, except by mystics. But it has always gone hand in hand with prosperity attitudes. It is a seem-less part of the good, and Good Guy, life.

On the other hand, this suggestion of giving service won't be easy at first. Procrastination will set in, given the overburdened time frame in which you already work. Like going to the gym, you'll have to "force" yourself to volunteer and keep it up. Don't bite off more than you can chew and don't attempt to save the world in a day. Just give a couple of hours of your time.

Turning to number 19, we enter a different area of thought and behavior. Differentiating between ambition and greed is no easy matter. We are taught to prize a faster buck, to move up the ladder of success with breakneck speed. Is this ambition (a good thing)? Or is it greed (a bad thing)? And how do you tell the difference? Here are some observations on practicing the method.

Do not regard yourself as either a greedy *or* an ambitious person. They both live in all of us. View yourself as you ap-proach each situation. You may be asked to join a partnership, invest in a new venture, hire a person because of connections with influential individuals. If you find that you are rushing to change your prior strategy, to amend your plans and breath-lessly seek this golden opportunity, you are more than likely acting out of greed. On the other hand, if the opportunity ap-pears to be another step in accelerating your overall plan, a pro-pitious fit, a nick-of-time savior to accomplish original goals, you are acting with ambition.

Greed takes, but ambition achieves. Achievement requires goals. If the opportunity fits with your stated goals—take it! If it's for an extra short-term buck, stay away.

TO DO

List your goals, and make it a big list. Don't leave any goal out—even the foolish ones. Go back over the 20 guidelines and see how they each can be employed in achieving those goals.

MORE TO DO

Write a paragraph about your current most difficult situation, problem or decision.

_____

_____

_____

_____

_____

Adopt an on-the-give attitude. Imagine that you want to get nothing for yourself out of the situation. How would you act? What would you decide? How would you take the pressure off yourself in order to help others?

Example: I have to move my office and I am concerned about committing to a long-term lease. Initially, it sounds like a decision that affects no one but me. But, when I think like a Good Guy, I realize that the long-term office is closer to my kids' schools, and that, if I become a long-term tenant, my employees will see me as making a true commitment to the business. Scared as I am to take the plunge, I'll do it.

Is the new lease a wealthbuilding decision? Now that I reflect on it, I never saw a wealthy nomad.

CHAPTER 2

◇

Following Your
Road Map to the Top

Are you ready to get rich? That question may be more difficult to answer than it first seems.

It can be unnerving to find something that really changes your life—even for the better. The Good Guy method does, and it's very simple to follow. It is so simple, in fact, that you might ignore it. All you need is to do small, continuous, acts of graciousness, caring and generosity—every day, in as many ways as possible, without fail. And no one need know your plan to be a Good Guy. You can continue to sell, sell, sell or whatever your present situation requires.

Good Guyism Is Actually a Philosophy, an Attitude and a Behavior Pattern

The Good Guy philosophy is simple: Live on-the-give, without seeking rewards, and the rewards will come. Stated this way it seems otherworldly, akin to the teachings of Christian mystics like Catherine Ponder and other gurus of prosperity thinking.

15

The difference is that the philosophy is transformed into astounding material success through certain attitudes displayed by every millionaire we have known.

- They are patient.
- They are goal driven, not materially driven.
- They are long-term, not short-term thinkers.
- They would rather build an organization than a bank account.
- Satisfaction comes with giving, not getting.
- They want to be remembered for something more than wealth.

Are these your attitudes, too? Probably they are, but you were taught that they would *not bring rewards*. The Good Guy method teaches otherwise.

Being a Good Guy is like making money in the stock market. You are what you do, not what you think. If you pick the right stock and don't buy, you don't achieve success. If you have Good Guy intentions and don't act on them, you are not living on the give. Good Guy behavior shows up in the letters you write, in the complaints you handle, even in the computer software you choose. You'll see.

Whether you're a secretary or a CEO you're probably familiar with the latest business buzzwords—"caring and giving." Bumper stickers suggest that you "Do random acts of kindness." You may find your CFO and VP holding hands on a tightrope during a "teamwork weekend."

However, no motivational trainer can teach you that true goodness starts in your own little room, in your own little chair and in your own gut. If you're going to become a big success by reading this book, and you easily can, you must be a genuine Good Guy. You probably can't fake it to make a buck. So, if you are really a bad guy trying to acquire the latest fashionable selling tool—a giving heart—forget it. We genuine Good Guys have too big a lead.

Why a Good Heart May Have Been a Handicap, and How To Turn It into Newfound Wealth

Many genuine Good Guys have not found the success they deserve. Some fall into the trap of undercharging for their services, doing too many favors, hiring losers and generally defeating their own efforts. The ultimate, ironic result of this behavior is that they are often not seen as Good Guys at all. Why? Because if you feel—even as a result of your own decisions—that the world is taking advantage of you, you build up resentment, not love. *The result of undercharging is palpable resentment toward the customer and ultimately a failing business.*

Generosity of Spirit is a beautiful part of being a Good Guy. But don't confuse it with "patsy" or "soft touch" behavior.

"Resentment" marks the difference between Good Guy behavior and doormat behavior. People who have toed the line, been mother's little helper, and made the coffee are not necessarily Good Guys poised for success. *They are often folks with low self-esteem.*

The good news is that you can easily change your better nature into a success machine. Your generosity should be given not to manipulate, or to gain gratitude, but because, like Mount Everest, the good deed is there to be done.

◇

HOW TO USE THE TIPS, HOW-TOS AND OPPORTUNITIES IN THIS BOOK

Each chapter is divided into four parts. First, you learn the details of practicing the Good Guy method in your everyday life as expressed by Milt or Adriane in Chapters 2, 10, 11 and 12. Second, Adriane explains how she used the method to improve her own business. Next, you answer your own Silent Survey to get you started. Finally, you take action.

With daily practice of the many Good Guy "how-tos" and "to-dos" you will develop a sixth sense of how to handle any situation to make the Good Guy system work toward significant wealth. And while you are doing this you *must* chronicle your efforts. Keep your own Good Guy journal to remind you of where you have been and where you are going in implementing the methodology.

Throughout this book you will find a device that Adriane has used in many financial planning books with very positive response from readers: the "Silent Survey"—questions you ask and answer yourself, without pressure and without any right or wrong responses. They help you identify both your resistance and your best approaches to Good Guy techniques. You encountered your first Silent Survey in Chapter 1.

SILENT SURVEY #2

Please answer these questions:

- Do I think of myself as a good person, a soft touch, a tough guy?
- Which self-image pleases me the most?
- Who are my heroes, my success models? How would I characterize them?
- Do I feel pushed around, "too good," a victim?
- Why? When?
- In my heart, do I believe that nice guys finish last? Am I ready to try it the opposite way?
- What first step of the many suggested in Chapter 1 will I take in the next hour?

Write down your first Good Guy idea. Do it.

Often, genuinely wonderful people resist their own good nature because they feel too inferior, too timid and too vulnerable to be openly nice. Others believe they have nothing to give the world, and still others fear that the world will take advantage of them. No, No, No!

If you have been given the remarkable gift of a loving heart, if you can understand what others are feeling and help them, *do it. Don't hide your gift of goodness.* That's a "failure" thing to do.

For now, here are some of the things you can do today to enrich yourself by enriching others. Start them even before you finish reading this book.

The Behavior Bible for the Daily Enrichment of Others

As with every new self-discipline, the first step is the hardest. Milt would say, "the first step brings you half way there." The Chinese philosophers would say, "A journey of a thousand miles starts with the first step."

Your behavior bible is nothing more than a restatement of many of Milt's 20 basic rules, with some further development added by you. After each on-the-give suggestion, list at least three ideas you have for implementing the notion, in a way that fits your own business or endeavor. Then you can start your own Good Guy Journal with the worksheets at the end of the chapter.

• Send Immediate Help—After nearly every mail, telephone, or personal business or professional contact, send the individual something in the mail within 24 hours. It may be an idea, a clipping or evidence of an action that you took on their behalf. But it must be in the interest of the recipient and not in the interest of your gaining business yourself.

This is not a bribe or a material gift. Except around the holidays, giving pens, pencils, or wine, means that you are not interested enough to discover the person's real needs, so you send something expensive instead. Keeping records of hobbies, charities and predicaments (for example, moving, looking for a good piano teacher for a child, or a bad back) of your clients and associates is a valuable tool. Some might use the phrase "hot button." We say, identify and fulfill your associates' "needs."

It might be just a matter of interpretation, but what a different message you give to the world!

Ideas: _____

_____

_____

• Give Networking Help to Others—Ask for multiple business cards. Always ask for more than one card and explain that you will distribute it to others if a third party can benefit.

Ideas: _____

_____

_____

• Give Your Attention—During any new business or professional contact, focus the spotlight on the other guy. Write down what is said, ask questions, learn about the individual. Avoid the temptation—even if asked—to emphasize your success, your values, your business. Questions will afford you more time from others, and you are more likely to open a door for the future.

Ideas: _____

_____

_____

• Give Justified Praise—Generously give praise or approval to individuals or businesses who have performed well, even where there is no immediate commercial or professional benefit in sight.

Ideas: _____

_____

_____

• Give Your Punctuality—Begin the habit of delivering faster than promised or expected. In a world filled with deadlines, Nice Guys give a high priority to schedules for the benefit of others.

Ideas: _____
_____
_____

• Give a Little Something More Than Expected—Discipline yourself to enrich others by delivering A, B, C and D when only A, B and C were promised. Watch the results! The additional effort is not a gift or a discount, but extra service, care or consideration for the needs of others.

Ideas: _____
_____
_____

• Give Yourself Accessibility—Be there for the world: Teach a course, give time (not just money) to charity, help a subordinate. Invest some of your valuable time in guidance and training of colleagues, teaching school classes, or helping students or young people seeking careers.

Ideas: _____
_____
_____

• Give Your Courtesy—When you hand others your business card, write the date, occasion and a few noncommercial words as a reminder of help that is available with "no strings attached." Send thank-you notes for services well done (don't wait until Christmas). Send a confirming summary of every important meeting and conversation. This is not only a courtesy but also a fail-safe prevention of misunderstanding and an opportunity to send a carbon copy that will impress and inform a third party. Watch your list of admirers grow!

Ideas: _____

_____

_____

• Give Your Opinion—Write a letter to the editor of a magazine or newspaper at least four times a year. The letter should refer to a topic of current interest: Provide added information; state a conclusion or call for action; and sign with your name, address and phone number. With each letter published you are more recognized and useful to the world.

Ideas: _____

_____

_____

• Give Your Congratulations—Give to a favorite charity in honor of a milestone event of any business, social or professional contact. This may be for a birthday, wedding, graduation, confirmation or bar mitzvah. Your world will be both enriched and impressed.

Ideas: _____

_____

_____

• Give Your Money—Always share the wealth when it starts pouring in, even if it is not promised or required. Your colleagues, associates, employees and family deserve a "piece of the action." Enriching their lives is part of your continued investment.

Ideas: _____

_____

_____

If you've ever attended a training seminar or browsed through bookstores for management and/or sales books, you'll recognize the Good Guy Behavior Bible as the homespun counterpart of many best-sellers such as: *In Pursuit of Excellence, The One Minute Manager, Finding the Giant Within You,* and more. The Good Guy method combines and nurtures all these separate pearls of wisdom.

The prolific writer Isaac Asimov, in his autobiography, *In Memory Yet Green,* wrote: "Life goes on minuta by minuta." And some pursue this philosophy with great success. Excellence is pursued one attention-getting phone call at a time or one Good Guy act at a time. And etiquette—the simplest yet most powerful tool—comes first. It is polite, not pushy, to explain who you are and how you learned about the recipient of your business card. It is less taxing for the recipient, and it will probably generate business for you. Yes, a whole world of networking skills can be synthesized in the single word, "polite." It is polite to listen, for example, or to send material to a home if it is more convenient for others.

Today, these listening and networking skills are often discussed in terms of "guerilla tactics," or "super-sales techniques." Companies spend fortunes on neurolinguistic training and body language, whereas the Good Guy seeks old-fashioned empathy and attention to fellow human beings.

Etiquette comes into play even in the touchiest and most difficult of circumstances—hiring and firing a relative. Countless sleepless nights and feuds are engendered by families who are in business together. Amy Vanderbilt or Miss Manners is the best mentor. It's not nice to mislead individuals, to open their expectations to wealth without effort, and then expect excellence. So don't do it. Be sure that you and your family member, employee, associate, or partner have an understanding of the ground rules.

Work habits for the Good Guy aren't very different from those of any conscientious person. Dreary as it may sound, do the work first; shoot for excellence and then some; read in your field and do your homework.

Also, part of Good Guy work habits is to tell the truth. Good Guys don't try to squirm out of a jam or find scapegoats; and they don't lie. This means that their work life must be particularly punctual, smooth operating, as free of crisis as possible. Their work habits must be designed and executed to avoid situations that tempt them to cover up, evade and fabricate.

Just prioritizing and not falsely promising to do the impossible will reduce your stress by half. Being a Good Guy does not mean overextending yourself to the point at which you resent every promise or are forced to leave half of them unfulfilled.

You might have thought that ethics would be the first consideration for the Good Guy; however, ethics is subject to interpretation and debate. We go by one golden rule: If it feels wrong to you, don't do it. Obviously, you must know right from wrong. Fortunately, even in this world of make-it-up-as-you-go-along ethics and where "everybody does it" seems like a valid excuse, there are easy-to-find standards. Those standards are found right in your gut. With just a few minutes' reflection, they're there.

You might also be surprised to find the admonition against buying or selling on the cheap in the category of ethics. Anyone in business for a long time will tell you that no one can uniformly deliver the best for less—maybe once in a while but not consistently. A few large retailers can undercut prices, but most eventually fold in the attempt.

For Your Good Guy Method Journal

Every day, fill out this chart until the gives become second nature to you:

What I Gave and What I Owe

Today's Date:

What I Gave:

Person, Group or Contact	Gift, Thank You, Special Help, etc.
Business Cards I Received	To Whom I Can Pass One On?
Item of Interest I Came Across	Whom Would It Help?

What Act of Charity, Grace or Kindness Did I Perform?

What I Owe:

Person, Group or Contact

What Is Owed and by What Date

(Review your notes for the day and fulfill the next day or on scheduled day.)

SILENT SURVEY #3

Ask yourself this question: How did I respond to the above Good Guy Behavior Bible?

Did I think the rules were babyish, routine, good ideas, easy to do, impossible, time consuming, simple to implement, or other? Go down the whole list again and answer separately for each suggestion. Remember that these are your answers and reactions and there is no right and wrong.

Many of you will react positively right from the start. All you need is economical and time-effective methods in order to implement your in-office Good Guy system. (We'll cover this in Chapter 3). Get a head start now:

To Implement the Gives, Here Are Five Things That Would Fit My Business, Job or Personal Career:

1. _____
2. _____
3. _____
4. _____
5. _____

Others who react positively in the Silent Survey may need a little creativity to get started:

Take a Good Guy Inventory of Your Workday

Give some thought to how most of your day goes. Whom did you meet with? Speak with? Write to? What type of stationary would help you institutionalize your gives? Here are three real-life ideas for implementing Good Guyism, but there are thousands:

- A dentist had a reminder card designed to include a sugar-free lollypop. When a client makes an appointment, within 24 hours the office sends a card with place, date, directions from the center of town and the lollypop.

- An authors' escort in Denver makes use of a souvenir pen featuring a moving stagecoach, which she buys at the Garden Of The Gods gift shop. There is no name on the pen, but it is mailed with every invoice. The authors' escort does it because she derives pleasure from giving away the lovely pen, and her invoices are now paid 30 percent faster.

- A firm implements the rule of summarizing each meeting by utilizing a preprinted form. During the course of the meeting, the lawyer who is in charge summarizes the data, which the secretary can immediately type out and mail. No extra work, but lots of efficiency.

Some, after taking the Silent Survey, may feel negative and resistant to the Good Guy concept. Or it may seem childish, or self-evident or Pollyannaish. Regardless, it works. Often we rationalize our own self-sabotage as good judgment or caution. We hold ourselves in reserve and dare not give too much to the world. When we do this, we often accept mediocre results, knowing that there is much more we can give to the world and get from it.

Ultimately, the Silent Survey may reveal that you have been preconditioned to think that getting ahead means being a Bad Guy. Whatever our individual experience, we seem to share a cultural barrier—a collective, deep-seated belief that prevents us from gleaning all the rewards that life has to offer. We believe, with baseball great Leo Durocher that "Nice guys finish last."

The best advice is to give the Good Guy method a try. Before long, *you will no longer send out to each new contact invisible signals that assert "give me your time," or "give me your business," or "give me your money," or "give me your confidence and approval."*

Unfortunately we send out the strongest "on the take" signals when we are the most needy, doing poorly financially, just starting out, or in other ways feeling like the underdog. However, Generation X looking for a first job, baby boomers struggling to make up for lost time, women newly in the workforce, veterans trying to break through the glass ceiling, and seniors seeking a second career all have incredible bounty to give to the world. So, it can be hardest to join the Good Guy program when we actually need it the most—when we might otherwise feel that the world has failed us.

Start anyway. Make a daily progress chart of the new Good Guy techniques you are integrating into your life. At the end of each day, ask yourself four questions, and do it throughout your business life:

1. How many chances to be a Good Guy did I have today?

2. How many did I miss?

3. How can I improve my record tomorrow?

4. What could I have gained for myself by helping others?

And before you turn off the lights on each business day, write out thank-you notes to everyone who was a Good Guy to you that day. And don't forget to mail them!

CHAPTER 3

◇

Selecting, Enriching and Empowering Your Good Guy Team

How Good Guys Get More Help from Their Staffs by Enriching Employees

This is a warning!

Despite your superior skills, energy and experience, you could become a victim of your own success!

Here's the danger: You become successful after exceptional effort and preparation in your chosen field. Business growth or promotion follow, and you suddenly become responsible, for the first time, for the hiring or performance of others. You are completely unskilled in this function, and your company or career go downhill.

This scenario is not uncommon. Here are a few typical true-life tragedies.

- A brilliant architect found his practice expanding rapidly as a result of lucrative new business and design opportunities. Unfortunately, he indiscriminately hired draftsmen, junior architects, office help and a support staff. Because the employees were mediocre, disorganized, demoralized, and a liability to the practice, the architect's business and reputation went downhill and never recovered.

- An exceptionally skilled surgeon depended exclusively on a medical employment agency for receptionists and book-keepers. He had a series of them, to whom he paid little attention. He never interviewed or supervised. He was too busy with a practice that grossed over $1 million annually, and he also was on call to lecture at medical conventions all over the world.

  One conscientious bookkeeper at the start gave time and effort beyond normal expectations. Dr. X never noticed or appreciated the extra contribution at all. In resentment, the bookkeeper began embezzling small sums. As she found she was unsupervised and unnoticed, she increased these sums. Finally, when one large bill went unpaid and Dr. X started looking, he found traceable embezzlement over a period of 17 months of $288,000.

- An energetic salesperson left his boss and built a chain retail business. During rapid growth, he expanded the staff but retained total decision-making authority in all areas, including many growing departments and functions. He literally ran everything.

  After carrying excessive burdens for years without the benefit of secondary management, the owner was suddenly overwhelmed when a minor illness took him out of the office for a few days. Because nobody else was available to sign checks, make buying decisions or handle the daily stream of normal business problems, he suffered a nervous breakdown.

Some years ago, after witnessing many such situations in which great entrepreneurs had no back-up, Milt asked a workshop of business executives: "How do you rate yourself, on a scale of 1 to 100, in the overall performance of your own job?" These men and women were talented and successful, and most of them wrote down a figure of 90 percent or better.

Then they were asked: "Think of all the people working for you, and give me, on a scale of 1 to 100, a performance rating for them." Most of the responses came back with ratings of 45 to 85, and the averages were in the 60s.

The next question: "Can you make more money upgrading your own performance from 92 percent to 93 percent in the next year, or upgrading all your other employees' performance from 65 percent to 85 percent?" The group universally agreed they could make more money investing in their employees, instead of enhancing their own performance another point or two.

Now the crushing question: "Do you constantly concentrate on and strive to improve your own performance, or do you have a meaningful system to train, motivate, and upgrade your employees who can make you happier, healthier, and richer?" The majority confessed that they were still centered on their own performances, and did not have ongoing programs for the more significant, results-oriented upgrades of their employees.

Why do they overlook such a priority?

- *Habit.* Self-made professionals and entrepreneurs became successful through their own personal efforts. That's what they know best, and that's what they work on.
- *Ego.* There is a personal satisfaction in doing a job well, and some of this is lost when the priority shifts to schooling others.
- *Lack of vision and know-how.* The architect knew how to build great buildings. But he didn't know how to build a great staff, and he never learned how vital this was to commercial success. He is not alone in this weakness.

Is there a solution? Yes! In this chapter are the basics, which come from experiences of happy adventures and unexpected tragedies over decades. These five basic rules can be applied immediately by any manager in any company.

How Good Guys Hire
(and Cut Down the Need to Fire)

1. Never Hire in a Hurry

I learned this from my brother and lifetime business partner Larry Gralla, who cautioned me after I did it several times. I was on my way to a major trade show, and our magazine that covered this industry was missing a very key and important employee. Although I had a mediocre candidate, I was desperate to hire him and take him along. Larry told me: "I urge you to hire somebody for the next 20 years, not the next 20 days!" He was right! In the long run, the patient search for the right person is infinitely more valuable than the hurried decision to fill a critical empty slot.

2. Never Stop Looking

Qualified individuals with great potential often come along when you have no openings. See them anyway. Pass the word among employees, suppliers, and others that you or your company will always have the door open for the right person. Interview and stay in touch with anyone who looks good.

3. Recent References Are More Important
Than Old Job Listings

Never hire without checking references, and find out what the applicant has been doing recently, as compared with many years ago. Also, check references by phone rather than mail, and, after some routine questions, ask whether the former employer would rehire. In confidence, not to be repeated, determine the strengths and weaknesses of this individual.

4. The Applicant's Record Is Key

The "win versus lose" history is more vital than his or her work skills. Find out if this individual is achievement-oriented rather than someone who explains or complains why a previous job or challenge did not work out.

5. Never Overstate the Benefits of Your Job Opportunity

Excessive promises are the seeds of future discontent. Give a truthful picture of the demands, requirements, and opportunity of your job opening. Make it sound difficult and demanding; the fallout will leave you with quality survivors.

Good Guys Train Constantly, One Skill at a Time

Job training should be deliberate and continuous. Convey a general description, but teach one skill at a time. Be sure that the new employee applies learned skills immediately, or they will be forgotten. Supervise good performance at skill A before proceeding to skill B.

Learning is an endless progression.

After many years of conducting enriched three-day "sales meetings" for some of the more important members of our staff, we found that, as we noted earlier, most of the learned skills were not used and quickly discarded. We then began a program of training "one skill at a time" throughout the year. Employees concentrated on a single topic and were immediately supervised on its application. What a difference!

Good Guys Reward Excellence

There should be good adhesive to retain and motivate "above-average performers." This is as much of a problem as dealing with sub-par performers (see Chapter 4). The adhesive should include recognition and approval, new challenges, financial rewards, bonuses, raises, and profit sharing.

The Single Most Powerful Personnel Tool It Took Milt 15 Years To Learn

For many years I diplomatically delivered (so I thought) constructive and helpful guidance to above-average performers. Example:

"Joe, I'm proud of the way you and your staff handled the recent NSGA Show. Your enthusiasm and follow-up were exceptional. But, after three weeks, nobody has turned in the mailing list changes we need. It's not glamorous, but we can't let the list go stale. Here's a batch of forms; we need the changes."

One day I got some advice from my wife and lifelong helpmate Shirley, who is a truly inspired amateur psychologist. It had to do with "unqualified support of positive behavior." In other words, leave out the "but" . . . or save the constructive criticism for a separate and unrelated conversation. Examples:

"Marcia, I treasure the day we put you into a job only men had been handling. You're teaching these guys a lesson or two, and you've inspired the company."

"Joe, you've met every deadline despite working shorthanded with your department. We've noticed it and won't forget it. Thanks."

"Alan, I'm glad I gave up a piece of my job and turned it over entirely to you. You're doing great; I should have done this two years ago!"

Unqualified support of positive behavior (without the "but") has two magical qualities:

1. It sentences your employee (subconsciously) to continue that outstanding performance *forever!*
2. It opens the door to delivery of constructive criticism at another time.

Good Guys Make the Rules of the Workplace Absolutely Clear

In directing employees, Good Guys always differentiate between opinions and orders. Sooner or later, you run into trouble if you do not draw a clear line between personal advice and company requirements.

(A) "Jim, if I were in your shoes, I would handle that project this way. Listen to my views for a few moments, but then you're free to handle it whatever way you think best."

(B) "Dan, our company has rules and a specific system and format for the handling of this particular project. You can handle it in this standard way, or you can come back and tell management whether and how you propose to modify the system. But you are not free to make changes arbitrarily on your own."

Good Guys don't keep their employees guessing; they put the company rules in writing. Any company or professional practice, regardless of size, should have written rules for the workplace. These rules normally include security, punctuality, visitors, phone use, mail and materials handling, safety, and matters unique to that particular enterprise. Casual disregard of normal rules, even if minor, should be noted and corrected. Moreover, it is demoralizing and corrosive to allow rules to be systematically ignored by a few employees who consider themselves privileged.

Good Guys Discipline Their Employees

1. Do not encourage, solicit, or tolerate employee participation in behavior that is fraudulent, unethical, or illegal. If you don't understand or follow this rule, you might also ignore the rest of this book.

2. Try to establish a mutually agreeable deadline for any important project or plan discussed with any staff member. At the end of any such conversation, use a calendar, establish a reasonable deadline, and write it down in the presence of your staff member. This works wonders in keeping important projects and plans on target.

Warning: Key Employees Innocently Attempt To Erode Your Authority

What would you do if a key and valuable employee approached you as follows:

"Milt, I know your rule about no vacations without your personal OK between Labor Day and Thanksgiving, when we are all so busy.

"However, I'm planning a great family vacation to Disney World for ten days at the end of September. I got a super deal on air and hotel arrangements, by signing in advance, and my family is very excited about the trip.

"I know I'm giving you little notice, but I'll make it up to you when I get back. The guys in the office have promised to pitch in. So I'd like to have your approval for this trip."

Most employers have two basic reactions to this request. Either they refuse to break the rules, or they give an OK because of the great value and excellent longtime performance of this particular employee. But neither of these responses is entirely adequate. Here's a better reply.

"Harold, you have really asked me not one question but two questions. So I'm going to handle them one at a time.

"The first question is: 'Who is running this business?' Somebody has to make the rules, retain authority, and run the company in a way that is beneficial to all our employees and customers. So the first question is, who has that job, you or I?"

Now Harold must concede that Milt is running the business, and that's the only acceptable answer to that question.

"Now Harold, once we've established that I'm running this business, the second question is whether you are going on this trip.

"It appears you *are* going on this trip. You told your family, you bought the tickets, and you told your fellow employees about all the arrangements. Since I can't change any of that, you have prevented me from making any decision. The answer is that you are going, and that since you never asked me for an OK in time, I didn't give a decision.

"Harold, you're a very valuable guy here, but you may never again challenge my authority to run the company. You have used up your lifetime quota of doing this, and I'm going to let you and everybody else know about it."

This response may be softened to avoid alienation of a virtually irreplaceable employee. However, your authority is a more important asset than any employee who attempts to break the rules arbitrarily and get away with it.

What Good Guys Owe and Give to All Their Employees

- Truthful outlook during recruitment interviews
- Continuous (versus quickie, one-shot) training in job skills
- Written and fairly enforced rules of the workplace
- Achievement recognition whenever deserved
- Rewards and challenges for above-average performers
- Freedom from burdensome and demoralizing nonperformers (see Chapter 4 on this topic)
- Sense of team effort and purpose

———————◇———————

GOOD GUYISM APPLIED: ADRIANE DISCOVERS THAT AN HONEST JOB DESCRIPTION CAN CREATE A BIG COMPANY FAST

When I needed to hire personnel for my newsletter, I wanted someone to help with customer service, publicity and advertising. Because I had done all of it myself, up to then, I saw this as the job of one very qualified person.

A potential disaster was brewing. Typical of an entrepreneur, I was looking for a clone, not an employee. After I had carefully written down a detailed job description, I found tasks that clearly fell into three separate categories, suitable for people with different skills and interests.

I hired three people—two part time and one on a per-appearance basis to book publicity interviews. The total cost was slightly more than for one full-time employee, but the results were fantastic. My tiny partnership turned into a business with three departments, instead of the operation of a "one-armed paper hanger" with one exhausted helper.

Co-Opt Outside Help into Your Training Scheme

I wrote (and am still refining) my customer service training manual. Along the way, it occurred to me that both my data base company and printer should have a copy. In that way, they could coordinate better with the people in my office. Consider sharing your by-laws (see below) and other in-house documents with suppliers and others who service you. It makes for good communication.

SILENT SURVEY #4

Please answer the following questions:

1. How many people work for you in number?
2. How many people work for you in spirit?
3. Are you consistent with your rules?
4. Do you hold defined-time training sessions, or is training on the run?
5. Do you believe your employees to be loyal? Why? Why not?
6. How many days can the business run in your *total* absence?

7. How fast could a new employee become assimiliated into your business structure and office culture?

TO DO

Write a detailed job description for every job you need filled, including the ideal requirements for each position. If a sunny disposition means more than computer skills, admit it. Make demands on paper, then translate them into the job description you give to candidates. Remember that Good Guys don't lead candidates on by painting their workplace as a summer camp.

Now write such a description for jobs already filled. Do your present employees really qualify?

TO DO

Look in the mirror. Ask yourself, "Do I plan to give pensions, rewards, and other benefits to my employees?" If you don't, you may make money but you will never be an unbridled success. Rewarding a valuable employee is building your *own* future. If you don't value your employees enough to watch them grow with the company, perhaps it's time to look at your staff and make changes. Good Guys do not keep employees who don't deserve to get rich alongside them.

TO DO

Write a training manual for your company, no matter how rudimentary. If you have no employees as yet, write one for yourself! If you are the manager of many, review your present (perhaps elaborate) training program. Does it train one skill at a time? Does it call for immediate implementation? If not, try training the Good Guy way and see the difference.

TO DO

List any documents that you think should be shared outside your company to help related businesses deal more effectively with your employees and in-office systems.

Since the single greatest tool in retaining above-average performance is the unqualified recognition of any exceptional accomplishment, announce the good work of your staff to others. The employee of the month, year, etc., should be announced to your suppliers, customers and others. Include a profile in your newsletter (see Chapter 8). Or just fax a note to an A list of close business acquaintances saying, for example, "Jack Smith has just received his certification (went to school at night and graduated with top honors). What a guy! Next time you speak to him please remember that congratulations are in order."

Wait until Jack gets unexpected applause and finds out you took the time to sing his praises.

TO DO

Review the preceding paragraphs about recognition and write a set of company by-laws. Circulate them with a smile and an "I mean it" attitude.

TO DO

Create your own employee communication stationary. Here's an example:

FROM: You

TO: Your Receptionist

DATE: Today

RE: Card File Revision

To Do: Create two card files, one alphabetical, the other by type of company.

Date Due: Seven days from today

Detailed Description: Use our correspondence and filing system to identify type of firm. Take name from alphabetical list and look up file, identifying what kind of firm they are. Here is a list of possibilities: (give list). Ask Jane if you are not sure.

Trouble If Not Done: Harry can't create the data base I need for next month's mailing.

If Not Done on Time: May end up mailing in summer when things are slow for recipients.

Big Picture: Overall goal for which this task is essential is to do more direct mail selling.

CHAPTER 4

◇

Identifying and Resolving Employee Problems

Why Good Guys Act Humanely but Firmly To Recognize and Resolve Employee Failure

What would you do if a longtime employee with whom you share a personal friendship, and who was once a great asset, had tailed off so badly that you were convinced he could no longer perform the minimum requirements of his job?

What would you do if an employee with a job history dating back to being hired by your father had taken a smug attitude that he was invulnerable, and his job habits were affecting the morale of others?

What would you do if a talented and skilled employee was unable or unwilling to perform because of friction with others, and despite several efforts you had been unable to correct the situation?

The answers to all these problems are similar. But, first, here is a true story that demonstrates the importance of dealing with employee nonperformance.

Some years ago, during the last day of a business convention, I was leading a workshop on the topic, "How to get more help from your help." The participants were about 60 owner-managers or appointed executives of medium-size business enterprises.

I impulsively asked this question: "When you go back to your office Monday morning, imagine that an employee comes in and says 'I quit, Mr. Jones. I'm leaving in two weeks.'

"Most of you, in the case of the majority of your employees, would feel a sense of loss. But, now, think carefully. Is there anyone in the audience who, when confronted with the sudden resignation of a member of your staff, would have a sense of relief that the employee is leaving?

"In other words, are you 'carrying' anyone who you know has failed or will fail? If that is true of any of your employees, please raise your hand and stand up."

A few in the audience stood immediately. Others followed slowly. Most were waiting to observe the behavior of their peers. Eventually, nearly 40 percent stood up to confess that they were carrying at least one employee who had failed or would likely fail.

Why does an otherwise effective executive ignore and thereby perpetuate anyone's failure or likely failure? In my experience over the years, I find three basic reasons:

1. False hope that the situation will change. *(In truth, no change is likely without management intervention.)*

2. Guilt. Prosperous and successful people are saddened by the failure of others. Their guilt feelings prevent corrective action.

3. Fear. There is concern about legal ramifications as well as fear of "looking like a bad guy."

The single most vital step in resolving employee failure is to recognize the damage being done by an inept individual.

- He or she could be affecting the company's reputation, product, service, standards, and profitability.

- He or she is almost certainly affecting the work and morale of fellow employees.

- He or she is also hurting himself or herself. He or she probably recognizes the failing, but may not have the courage to take action.

Identifying such an employee problem is your job, and it must be handled immediately and courageously. Here's how:

First, arrange an immediate private meeting. (Let's call this individual Joe.) Invite Joe to give you a job description, as well as his own view of how he is performing. What are his strengths, weaknesses, and overall performance? As he responds, take notes, and then repeat his comments back.

Now it is your turn to cover the same ground. Describe Joe's strengths first, then his weaknesses. Conclude with any problems so troublesome that he and the firm must make a joint effort to bring his performance up to par.

If Joe complains or explains, you must be friendly but firm. You have a responsibility to Joe, to fellow employees, and the company, to bring his performance up to standard.

Describe your goals, and agree on a deadline. Because of the importance of the deadline, Joe should participate in setting it. If he complains, understand his point of view, but be firm in establishing an exact deadline. Write it down in his presence.

Now you can expect several possible outcomes.

In some cases (*and this is surprising*), Joe will resign immediately. He probably needs a fresh start, and recognizes that his making a change in your workplace is unlikely; he may have other motives. Whatever the reason, his resignation resolves the problem.

In some cases, he will give it a try, show temporary improvement, and then fall back to his old ways. This outcome is most frequent. But you will then find it easier to make the termination decision, because you and your firm have helped Joe give it a fair try—you have been clear and you are "on the record."

In a few cases, Joe will recognize that his poor habits have put him on dangerous ground, and he will reform permanently.

He will be an asset to you, his fellow employees, and himself. Such an experience of making a human life more positive and productive makes everything else worthwhile!

Before going on to the next chapter, ask yourself this question: "Is there anyone in my company whose resignation would bring me a sense of relief instead of a sense of loss?" If the answer is "yes," it is time to take action—for the benefit of your company, of your associates and fellow employees, and of the individual who is doomed to failure unless you act!

———————— ◇ ————————

GOOD GUYISM APPLIED: HOW ADRIANE LEARNED TO ENJOY THE ANNUAL REVIEW

As a lawyer practicing in a large New York firm for many years, I became well acquainted with the annual review. Twenty years of experience and observation later, I can attest that it is one of the most destructive forces to business success.

Yet, you must meet to review your employees' *future* performance. And there are ways of turning this negative to a positive and even enjoying the experience.

- Follow Milt's rules. If you are thinking of firing, don't wait until the annual review. Follow the procedure immediately. Annual review is not the time when "heads roll." An organization that sets that up will have a nonproductive workforce for at least the month prior.

- Again, follow Milt's rules. Annual review is not primarily for praise. That must take place consistently throughout the year. Good workers must be aware of your appreciation all along. They should not be "surprised" with their bonus or raise, even if it is awarded on a yearly basis.

- So, what do you do at the annual review? You don't review employees in general; you review the results of the projects on which they worked. Review them one at a time. What successes are to be repeated next year? What failures to be avoided? What new skills are left to learn? What creative ideas do they have?

SILENT SURVEY #5

Please answer these questions:

1. How many people have I fired in the last three years?
2. Why?
3. How can I improve my hiring practices to reduce firing?
4. Is there someone I want to fire?
5. What changes could the employee make to save the job? By when?

TO DO

Take a deep breath and set up your firm but fair meeting session.

CHAPTER 5

◇

Employing Relatives Without Grief: Overcoming the Hazards and Reaping the Rewards

Relatives in Your Business, on Your Payroll, or in Your Hair? Good Guys Get Rich with Their Kin . . . Careless Guys Lose It All!

What would you do if your married daughter Judy approached you privately after a family Sunday dinner, and said emotionally:

"Dad . . . I'm so upset about how you've been treating Lennie at the office. . . ."

"We just had a big argument . . . He's like a son to you . . . Can't you give more consideration to your own flesh and blood? . . . How can you treat someone this loyal like he doesn't even care?"

Judy tries to say more, but she starts crying.

Now, it happens that your son-in-law Lennie is becoming quite an asset to your company and has shown potential for management and a bright future. Like anybody, he makes mistakes, but he learns from them.

Judy is probably referring to an incident last week. Lennie failed to patch up another employee's botched work because he left for his usual Thursday night poker game. On Friday, you

49

had met Lennie and explained that management is a responsibility, not just a privilege. You told him: "Sometimes management requires personal sacrifice. We have to set an example for others, and we have to produce results . . . not explanations. I've never forgotten that, and I hope you'll remember it, too."

Lennie seemed to accept the talk, and he did not seem upset. You had no idea he had "taken the story home" to Judy.

Should you now (a) cool Judy off and tell her what really happened, and/or (b) advise her to stay out of family business, and/or (c) tell Lennie not to take business stories home, or (d) pursue some other course?

If you answered (d), make some notes before you finish this chapter. Then see rule #3 below.

What would you do if, after 10 months of sincere effort by all parties, you reached the inescapable conclusion that your nephew, Richard (son of your sister Mabel), would hurt both himself and your business by continuing his career in your firm? To make matters worse, Mabel was so justifiably proud of you and your prosperous business that she did a big selling job on Richard last year. He interviewed with you, left another job, and joined your firm with high hopes! And you thought dependable "family help" would be super, so you contributed your own support and enthusiasm!

Now you face big trouble—in your business if you let him stay on, or in your family no matter how you try to ease him out!

The solution to this one is the *first and most important* rule of this chapter. Make a note of your views before you read on! Then see rule #1.

The world is filled with many beautiful family business enterprises. Blood relatives peacefully share responsibility, loyalty, ownership, energies, and hope for continuity to the next generation. Because these qualities strengthen a business and its reputation, owners and entrepreneurs often hire sons, daughters, in-laws, brothers, cousins and others.

But high hopes are not always realized. If the relationship turns sour, the results are much more catastrophic than the simple failure of an unrelated employee. The results: lost momentum, family breakups, lingering lawsuits, bankruptcies, and family devastation ensuing from business disputes. There have even been tragic suicides in which family business conflict was a major factor.

A few basic rules will help anyone take full advantage of the multiple benefits of family business affiliations, while hopefully steering clear of the pitfalls and tragedies.

1. Always leave an escape hatch for either or both parties. Everyone hopes for a permanent and mutually rewarding relationship, but this does not always happen. Whose fault? Unimportant!

   All parties must admit at the start that there is no certainty of success. Each individual must feel free to "call it quits" without blame or explanation. Why endanger the health of the business or of the family because either party is afraid or embarrassed to call off an employment experiment?

2. Avoid premature promises of wealth, equity, and easy success. The family enterprise was built on energy, risk, dedication, creativity. It's much better to describe those needs to the new recruit than to promise a quick and simple trip to "easy street."

3. Both parties must agree to resist meddling and unwanted advice from family members not active in the business.

   Although well-meaning relatives are clearly outsiders, they often like to appoint themselves as an "advisory committee" on work schedules, job conditions or a variety of other job issues in which their experience is limited. Such interference must be dealt with the first time it occurs, to ensure that it doesn't happen a second and third time!

   A particularly important rule is to avoid serious business discussions at home. Let's go back to the story about the daughter who complains about how Daddy is treating her husband at the office. She should not get a reply in a family setting. Instead, she should be invited promptly to Dad's office, where she can repeat her "advice" but will also see him in a different perspective, as the head of the business. Discussions relating to business belong in the office or workplace. If permitted at home, these discussions invite the participation of emotional but unqualified relatives, who do more harm than good to a business operation.

4. Don't rush big money, benefits or "perks" to anyone whose importance to the family is greater than his or her early importance to the business.

Recipients of such generosity may subconsciously feel unworthy of these benefits. Some take it in stride, but others develop guilt, anger or overconfidence.

The enterprising head of the business very likely became a winner through patience and supreme effort—before seeing results. The same qualities must be encouraged in others.

5. If "perks" or benefits are given to a relative, such as a car, additional vacation time, bonuses or other "goodies," this must be done quietly, and not intentionally exposed to other employees not related to management.

Jealousies often poison the performance of otherwise capable employees. Envious employees can easily take a destructive dislike to otherwise capable executives who are relatives of the owner. So if goodies are extended, keep them low key and out of sight!

6. Put in writing what was promised and what was not promised. Be sure that you have an arbitration clause in any agreement, formal or informal, describing the affiliation of a family member in your business. Business-related disputes often endanger the original

well-conceived plan. If a legal battle follows, the great expense and diverted energy often erase hopes of family business survival.

Arbitration is faster, cheaper, less formal, and just as effective. Arbitration clauses are essential, and the sooner they are employed, the better for the firm.

7. Plan and initiate the professional progress of your relative in the business. A relative is seen as symbolic of the family business. He or she must develop and continue to grow professionally.

   Available training and development sources include trade associations, specialized seminars, trade shows and conventions, business or trade magazines in your field, and special supplier events. All of these are valuable and essential for any blooming leader.

   We live in a fast-changing world. No executive or entrepreneur should limit the learning opportunities of his relatives and future successors to the experiences available in the workplace.

8. Meet periodically to discuss performance, give compliments, set new goals.

   Often one party may have a great feeling of achievement, while the second party harbors, but does not voice, some frustrations or negative views. Even seemingly simple matters, such as late arrival time, casual abuse of expense funds, neglect of an important client, sloppy paperwork, or neglected priorities, can be sources of trouble if not voiced.

   Periodic reviews are essential, and both parties should have plenty of time for expression. Don't "keep it in" and wait for the explosion, because explosions often characterize a situation that is out of control.

9. Don't keep an obvious successor on the string too long. A common misjudgment by otherwise outstanding entrepreneurs involves the failure to empower a

successor. Most highly successful businesspeople are imaginative, dedicated and professional. However, they are unable to consider that (1) they are not scheduled to live and be healthy forever, and (2) anyone else in the world, however well prepared, can possibly handle the job that they are now doing. Behind them there is often a talented and impatient son, daughter, or son-in-law, or someone else on an eternal string. Here's what happens when promotion is avoided:

- Others in the organization lose respect for the second-in-command, since it is obvious that Daddy intends to call the shots forever.

- The heir-apparent becomes discouraged or embittered; some even leave, and the company loses a great potential for future leadership.

  Milt recalls typical instances in which a furniture chain, a prosperous remodeling company and a prominent wholesale firm were impacted negatively by father and son, brother and brother, or other relatives splitting up when increased management responsibility was withheld from qualified relatives. In each case, family members quit and started their own competitive firms. Both the established business and the new competition suffered!

- When unanticipated change at the helm takes place because of death or illness, it is much more threatening to the firm than orderly transition.

How To Agree on an "Escape Hatch" Before One Relative Employs Another

The pre-job discussion of an "escape hatch" must be introduced by the employer, but it's vital for the recruit to participate and agree. Here's how an ideal conversation might go:

Employer: "Donald, I'm as excited as you about your future here . . . but I must ask what are the odds that it will work out for you and for us?"

Recruit: "Uncle Phil . . . It's practically a sure thing . . . maybe 10 to 1!"

E: "Well, the numbers are unimportant . . . just as long as we agree that there's always an outside chance it may not work. These things happen. Now suppose one day you decide you can't succeed here, or you want to turn to another field, or you want to go back to your own field, or you're unhappy for any reason. What would you do?"

R: "Well . . . I guess I'd have to tell you."

E: "Right . . . and be sure to tell me first! Griping to someone else would hurt me, and you, and the business, and the family! Now suppose I don't think it's working out. What should I do?"

R: "Tell me first . . . I guess?"

E: "Right again! Donald, I'll be doing my level best to give you every boost for a great career here. But remember, I've got the same right you have to call it off. Agreed?"

R: "Okay . . . that sounds fair."

E: "One last thing, Donald. If either one of us ever decides to call it off, we don't blame anyone, we don't make excuses. We just call it a mutual decision, and we don't endanger the family, or the business, or your future, with useless faultfinding. Okay?"

R: "Okay."

E: "Then let's get going. This business needs you now."

What About the Wife or Husband Who Works Part-Time To "Help Out"?

How about the wife (or husband) who comes in to "help out" in a business because (a) it saves money at the critical start-up stages; or (b) it provides extra help for seasonal or other high-pressure needs of the enterprise; or (c) the spouse has some exceptional skills needed by the business.

While a whole book or chapter could be written on this topic alone, here are a few key suggestions that will work most of the time:

- Pay him (her) on the regular payroll, even if it involves some extra tax money. It's businesslike and emotionally supportive.
- Make the deal temporary and hire someone else when you can afford it—unless an exceptional and nearly irreplaceable skill is involved.
- Warn the spouse to maintain a friendly but arm's-length relationship with other employees.

In repeated instances, the boss's wife has become socially involved, too completely, with a favorite friend at the office. In one extreme case, Mrs. W. began shopping trips and social evenings with widow M., a middle manager. The friendship reached the level of exchange of private family confidences, whereupon M. began flaunting the friendship to other employees. When M. began assuming special privileges, the situation had reached the point of no return: There were a demoralized workplace, a husband blaming his wife, and two nice women wondering what had happened!

———————◇———————

GOOD GUYISM APPLIED: ADRIANE BRINGS BUSINESS ARBITRATION HOME

I am an arbitrator with the American Arbitration Association. Every state has enacted a law that permits binding arbitration. Once you agree to arbitrate, that agreement is enforceable, and any court actions can be stopped.

Arbitration works in family disputes, neighborhood disputes and in family businesses as well. Lawyers are not necessary. You can agree on a private tribunal made up of persons you choose, or submit your dispute to a major organization like the AAA.

In my book, *Financial Planning for Couples,* you can read about dispute resolution at home. The advice is to take money out of the bedroom and bring it into the boardroom, which applies to work discussions as well.

But don't be fooled, because such resolution is not easy. I've presided over the marital and business divorce of too many husbands and wives to feel glib about it.

For this chapter there are no Silent Surveys and no To Dos. Just realize this important lesson: The best person for your life is not necessarily the best person for your business.

◇

CHAPTER 6

Writing Letters That Get Results—Instead of Getting Tossed

"Giving" Letters Reach and Impact Decision Makers; Ordinary Letters Fill the World's Wastebaskets!

The simple personal letter represents a great opportunity for business success and growth. But this valuable tool often is neglected or done so poorly that it never gets serious attention from its target.

Good letters can make an impression, reach the "unreachables," open doors, and improve the sender's reputation as a "Good Guy worth answering." Yet, every day's mail is filled with letters doomed to be discarded either before they're opened or after the recipient has given them about three seconds. Here's what happens to business letters:

1. They are discarded without being opened. (Frequent.)
2. They are opened, scanned and discarded within seconds. (Most often.)
3. They are opened, read, but make no impact and stimulate no action. (Frequent.)
4. They are opened and read to the end; they make an impression. (Rare.)

5. They are opened, read and stimulate either a reply or action from the recipient. (*Very* rare.)

In many years of workshops with his staff, and later with business groups, Milt has asked salespeople, working owner-managers or executives why they don't or can't write more effective business letters. These are the replies.

1. "No time; too busy."
   (This is a cop-out. They really do have time and motivation to send effective letters. When the formula becomes habit, each letter flows and is not time-consuming.)

2. "It is not necessary; I keep in touch by phone."
   (This is another cop-out. Letters are more permanent than phone calls, and they allow you to reach third parties with copies.)

3. "I used to write letters, but they were not helpful."
   (Writer has never developed a habit or skill of writing effective letters.)

4. "I'm doing OK; I don't need it."
   (Moderate success is a curse. It closes the mind to new skills that accelerate success.)

Avoiding Loser Openings

Before starting a letter, remember that the recipient is very protective of his or her valuable time and attention, and will turn off unless the letter opening promises a tempting answer to the subconscious question: "What's in this for me?"

The target of your letter is not interested in your pitch, or in spending money, but is looking to solve problems, make progress, enrich his or her own life and business.

Three stale and nearly useless openings fail to compel readership in most letters Milt has examined over the past 30 years. Examples:

1. "Thanks for taking time out of your busy schedule to meet with me (talk with me) yesterday."
   (This opening offers nothing new, is too apologetic, is subservient, and reinforces the idea that the recipient did you a favor by giving you any time at all.)
2. "Confirming my previous proposal, we can supply . . . deliver . . . service . . . etc."
   (The recipient knows he or she will have to pay for what you are offering. You are opening the letter by putting your hand into the potential client's pocket).
3. "We are one of the best service and supply firms in your field."
   (Ugh! This is awful and throw-outable. This approach is used by otherwise gifted owners, executives, and sales persons. They just don't know how to open a letter.)

Benefit the Recipient with These Good Guy Openings

Here are three better ways to open a much more appealing letter to the recipient. Also, these openings make it easier to make the rest of the message more effective.

1. State what you did in the recipient's behalf since your last contact. In this connection, I recommend the word "after" as the first word in the letter. Here are two examples.

```
Dear X:
    After hearing about your new general
manager, Joe Martin, I am placing him
on our free newsletter mailing list and
sending him back copies of the newsletter
for the past six months.
```

Or

Dear X:

After our meeting I told Ms. Y about your changes in department Z. I also am sending to Ms. Y one of your business cards.

2. Send an enclosure. Example:

Dear X:

You asked about what's happening in government regarding safety rules, so I am enclosing some most recent news clippings and trade association reports.

Or

Dear X:

Here is a list of seminars, meet-ings, and trade shows coming in your field for the rest of this year. This might be useful to your son, Phil, whom I had the pleasure of meeting briefly yesterday.

Or

Dear X:

Your worries are over! Yes . . . the Basel Watch and Jewelry Fair has different April dates from year to year because of compliance with religious holiday dates. Enclosed are the dates of this Fair for the next ten years, which I just obtained from official sources.

(This is a true-life story! The recipient was a watch manufacturer, who soon afterward became a regular buyer of double tabloid page full-color advertising spreads in my National Jeweler *magazine.)*

3. Use the power of trivia to show the recipient you were really paying attention during your last conversation. Example:

```
Dear X:
    You asked about Larry Ganes, the long-
time Midwest rep for Miller Container. He
is retired in Arizona, and I am enclosing
his address. I'm sure he'd enjoy hearing
from you!
```

Once you have started a letter in a nonthreatening way that opens the door, you'll find the rest flows easily.

Briefly elaborate the benefits of the new action mentioned in your own opening paragraph. Examples:

```
    I'm certain that Ms. X will reach you
with useful information about subject Y
after I've sent her a separate letter and
your business card.
```

Or

```
    I'm confident that our newsletters
will help Joe Martin accelerate his
orientation in your company and in
this field.
```

Or

```
    The enclosed will provide the
information you were lacking on this
subject.
```

After you open with new information or an enclosure to the recipient, and then use the next paragraph or two to mention the benefits of your action, it is then OK to begin reviewing your previous business matter.

The prospect will be more open to this information. This also helps to alert involved third parties in your organization and in his. As we have said, it pays to distribute copies of your letter to affected third parties.

Now, here is one of the most often used but useless letter closings in American enterprise. It is a deathblow to further action, but in 30 years of reviewing actual letters, Milt has seen it repeated thousands of times:

"If there is anything else you need, please do not hesitate to contact me."

Your potential client has read this phrase thousands of times. It says nothing.

Instead of using such wording, you can be in the top 2 percent of effective business letters by using the magic letter-closing trick of *inviting the recipient to take further action in his or her own behalf.*

Examples:

1. "Is there anyone else in your firm who would benefit from receiving our free monthly newsletter? Please send me names and business cards, so that I can take care of this immediately."

2. "Enclosed is a list of technical, financial, or research people in our place who can be useful to you. You may consult anyone, at any time, with no strings attached. I hope you will save this list."

3. "I have some new data and reports coming June 1 on subject Y. Let me know if you'd like to receive them. There is no obligation."

If you want to develop the habit of writing letters faster, more easily and more effectively, start a file. Save copies of your early letters; make your own list of your best openings and closings. The world's influentials, unreachables and decision makers will treasure your thoughts, and will remember you positively instead of looking for the nearest wastebasket!

This Typical Mediocre Letter Is Discarded Quickly After You Turn on the Recipient's "Defense Mechanism"

Dear xxxxxxxxx:

Thanks for taking time out of your busy schedule for our pleasant meeting last Monday.

This is too apologetic, too late and totally devoid of new information.

Confirming my proposal, we suggest an initial order of XXXXXXXXXX and YYYYYYYYYY, which you are certain to find useful and profitable. I can schedule delivery before the end of the month if you confirm promptly.

This asks for money or business prematurely and teaches your prospect to say "no" to you.

We are now one of the fastest-growing suppliers in this field. Hope you won't pass up this opportunity!

You give nothing when you talk of yourself instead of your intended client.

If there is any other information I can provide, please do not hesitate to contact me.

This is the most useless closing in the annals of business letters.

Sincerely,

Steve Miller

This Letter Structure Delivers Attention and Progress When Opening and Contents Go "On the Give" to Recipient

Dear XXXXXXXXXX:

After our meeting this morning, I immediately placed your new associate, Jane Williams, on the mailing list to receive our free newsletter and periodic research reports.

Open by stating what positive new action you have taken since the last contact.

I'm also sending her a copy of this letter and the material mentioned above for the past 12 months. I'm confident this will help speed up her orientation and convince you both that your needs are our priorities!

Send a helpful enclosure to enhance this new action. Diplomatically translate this action into benefit(s) for the letter recipient.

I've made notes of the questions you raised, and on the next visit I'll be back with answers . . . but no order pad! No strings attached!

Set up the next contact as a further enrichment of the letter recipient.

Meanwhile, I'm enclosing a list of those in your company now on our complimentary mailing list. If you have any other associates who might benefit from our (noncommercial) news and research information, please let me know their names by mail, phone or fax.

Close by inviting prospect to take further action in his or her own behalf.

Sincerely,

Steve Miller
cc: Jane Williams

———————◇———————

GOOD GUYISM APPLIED: HOW ADRIANE USED GOOD GUY LETTER-WRITING HABITS TO HELP AVOID DISPUTES AND "WIN" ARGUMENTS

Before I practiced Milt's Good Guy letter-writing methods, I wasn't in the habit of jotting down information or committing conversations to writing. The Good Guy method forced me to be less "verbal" and to rely more on written material taken down at meetings and during conversations. The result was an interesting by-product.

My letters substantiate what was promised by me, and by the other guy, with outcomes and anticipations. My Good Guy letters are documents that we all can rely on, in the event of a future misunderstanding. As a lawyer, I always knew the value of putting things in writing. But I also saw it as a hostile, often aggressive thing to do. With the Good Guy method, each letter offers help, even if it also performs the function of recording deals, details, promises and conclusions.

On numerous occasions I have been able to avoid disputes and usually prevail in a misunderstanding because I take the time to write down and follow up a meeting with a letter or fax in the Good Guy style.

It's a habit to cultivate!

Adriane's Super-Pack of Good Guy Letters That Every Business Needs

There is a package of letters that you should draft immediately for your business. The faster you get them in your computer the better. They may include collection letters, sorry letters (things you goof up and need to correct), congratulations letters (thanking the customer after a purchase).

Decide on the letters right now. Here's my key list:

- Refund letters
- Customer service problem letters
- Welcome letters
- Failure to pay letters

In Chapter 11 on becoming an automated Good Guy, you will learn about software that helps draft letters for you. But there is no substitute for your personal touch.

SILENT SURVEY #6:

Please answer these questions:

1. Do you call or write more often?
2. Do you think writing is too time consuming?
3. Do you have a complete and accurate record of the business relationships, agreements and ideas created and developed with others?
4. Do you read all your mail?
5. Do you save the business letters you receive?
6. Do you save records of your phone calls?

The likelihood is that you forget your calls and read and save your letters. Point made.

TO DO

List the letters that would be useful to your business. Jot down a Good Guy word or two that your clients, customers or suppliers would appreciate:

1. To clients:
2. To customers:

3. To colleagues:

4. To suppliers:

5. To professionals:

6. To employees, partners and co-workers:

As Milt suggests, I tend to start every letter with the word "After"—"After I spoke with you I became interested in Shaker furniture. You certainly have an interesting hobby. Did you know that our town museum has two world-class Shaker examples? Call me and we can take a field trip."

Even routine letters can use a Good Guy outlook. Here are some examples that don't require genius levels of intelligence:

Dear Subscriber:

Enclosed you will find your refund. Please keep any issues you have received with our complements.

If you find the time, we would appreciate it if you would drop us a line as to how we could have improved our newsletter to your satisfaction.

Very truly yours,

Adriane G. Berg

P.S. Some folks learn best with books and audiotapes. Enclosed is a list of what we publish.

Dear Subscriber:

I was delighted that you wrote to me with your questions. I answered them in Issue No. __, Page__ of *Adriane G. Berg's Wealthbuilder Newsletter*. If you missed the answer, a reprint is enclosed.

Very truly yours,

Adriane G. Berg

Dear Subscriber:

After receiving wonderful letters of encouragement, I grow ever more enthusiastic about our newsletter. This is your newsletter, too. Please write with comments and questions.

As will always happen with any publication ordered toll-free and delivered by mail, there are details that must be completed. To keep the costs of the subscription down, I am trying to resolve all problems by mail. Simply see the list below. You'll find a check mark near the question that applies to you, with full instructions.

Thank you for your cooperation, and keep READING!!

Very truly yours,

Adriane G. Berg

CHAPTER 7

◇

Making Every Hour Count at Trade Expos, Shows, and Conventions

Reap Months of Wealth Gains in Just Days: How Good Guys Mine Golden Opportunities, Contacts at Trade Expositions, Meetings, and Conventions

If you're a would-be millionaire impatient with the pace of the climb to the top, this chapter is for you! Conventions and trade shows offer every energetic entrepreneur and businessperson a great opportunity to achieve six to twelve months of career progress in just three or four days!

Shows and conventions vary from a small, one-day event on a single floor at a nearby hotel to huge multiday expositions in massive convention halls of major cities, attended by thousands of national and international visitors. These events assemble, in one place at one time, an enriched opportunity for contacts, education, current and future resources, and other career "nutrition."

The wealth-generating ground rules in this chapter are based on a lifetime of attending hundreds of these events, exhibiting at scores of them, and staging many such shows under the banner of Gralla Conferences Inc., a subsidiary of Milt's publishing firm.

How can anyone grow 12 months career-wise in a few days? Milt has seen it happen often for those who are energetic, well prepared and well directed. Here's a capsule of the most important rules!

- Plan to tour the exhibits by priority, rather than by geography. Many visitors to big trade shows mistakenly take the easier path of touring the event section by section, aisle by aisle. Later they discover that, by the second or third day, many of the most important Big Guns they wanted to see have departed for home. The educated Good Guy gets a copy of the show guide with exhibitor locations before the show begins, makes a priority list, and energetically skips around the exhibit hall, covering contacts in terms of importance rather than by location.

- Collect multiple copies of important catalogs, trade association membership lists, business cards, seminar papers and research reports, etc. If you pick up only one copy for your own use, you're out of luck for the whole year during which you could have been a Good Guy distributing useful copies to business friends and new contacts. You score points with new and old business friends by being a helpful and resourceful Good Guy.

- Dictate or record your reports, notes and data every single night. There is gold in the information and potential follow-up opportunities that an energetic person brings back from a multiday trade show. You get a head start on the rest of the world when you collect, dictate and organize this material every single evening, before you become weary or forgetful.

- If you are attending the event with colleagues, or are an exhibitor, establish a fail-safe "message exchange" procedure so that, even at the largest of shows or conventions, you and every member of your staff stand out as being totally organized. While others are subdued by the bedlam of a huge event, the world out there sees your team as perfectly organized, is impressed, and remembers!

- Whenever you send important literature or catalogs to the show, break the shipment into two packages and ship them separately. This is essential "life insurance" for the success of your trip. Otherwise, one loss of a single shipment could nullify your very costly efforts at an important annual event.

- Bring along a good supply of the business cards of your colleagues, as well as your own. Whether they attend or not, your colleagues and their services could be valuable to many of those you meet at the show. You're a remembered Good Guy when you're well prepared!

- As an exhibitor or participant, never allow any staff member or colleague to eat, drink or smoke in the exhibit space. Sloppy or unprofessional exhibitor behavior will damage your image among numerous old friends and new prospects, many of them current or future industry leaders.

- Get a list of seminars and workshops early, and attend those of direct or even marginal interest. One good idea, resource, or trend noted at any such event will pay growth dividends for a whole year.

- Join trade associations. Their reports, research, services, lobbying, contacts and other activities give every member a precious head start over nonmembers. Trade associations are worth their membership dues many times over!

- Circulate to several evening social events, wear your show identification badge, and watch for worthwhile contacts you missed during the business day. Carry plenty of business cards and ask a lot of questions! The contacts made and information gleaned at such events are often more productive than those pursued on the convention or exhibit floor!

- Collect business cards, and write on every one of them! Sometimes memory is dulled by multiple contacts or by the refreshments imbibed during the evening! A business card with a few scribbled words is your sure reminder of a prospective useful new business contact, even if met only briefly!

- At every firm you contact, old or new, get acquainted with the second-in-command, instead of just pursuing the Top Gun. I overlooked this rule several years, and it cost me dearly! The individual you ignore this year may have the top title and a very good memory next year!

- Get acquainted with the business media—the magazines and newspapers—in your own field. The editors and publishers are a great source of new friends, information, contacts, publicity, speaking invitations, and other benefits to your career and business. They should have your card, and remember meeting you personally. Shows and conventions offer ideal access to these important media friends.

- Get acquainted also with the show sponsors or management. Every one is a power center, filled with information, ideas, future convention dates, booth availabilities, and just plain gossip important to your future. Leave and collect business cards at these power centers!

- Finally . . . *Behave yourself!* Trade shows and conventions, with thousands of energetic people far from home, sometimes become pitfalls to normally well-behaved businesspeople who get involved in highly inappropriate behavior. Don't lose control just because a lot of others are doing it. Your reputation is on the line, and your colleagues and fellow professionals have keen eyes and long memories!

Three Success Stories with a Message from the Annals of Past Trade Shows

1. *"Complaints Receiver" Card Converts a Disaster Into an Asset*

Marcia Wilson, customer service star of Miller Packaging Creations, received "good news and bad news" from the company's vice-president, Alex Parker.

The good news: She was appointed Miller's first female district sales representative ever, joining 17 male colleagues.

The bad news: She was assigned a Southwest territory that had deteriorated to ground zero because of the neglect and arrogance of her predecessor in the same territory.

Despite an attractive new series of colorful packaging products, Ms. Wilson encountered hostility and closed doors during her first month on the job. Before the whole Miller team departed for a big five-day national packaging trade show, VP Parker gave Wilson this sage advice: "Forget about pushing the new line. Everyone you want to see is at the convention. Listen a lot. Get your foot in the door. Make yourself useful."

On her first day at the show, Wilson found more bottled-up hostility whether she met past customers at her exhibit, in the aisles, or at their exhibits. That night she pondered carefully the minds of Miller's alienated customers, who controlled her destiny.

Early the next morning, Wilson visited a "speedy printer" shop and had her business cards reprinted. Replacing the line which read "Southwestern District Manager," she printed "Southwestern Complaints Receiver." That day, she handed the card, with a smile, to *every contact* before saying a word!

The results were immediate. After a chuckle, Wilson began taking notes from important ex-customers now willing to give her time and attention. She heard and noted an unending history of broken promises, ignored service needs, delayed deliveries and careless mistakes. She carefully repeated the complaints, promised action, gave out cards and declined to "push" her attractive new line.

For the next few days, Wilson encountered open doors, top-level executives who were no longer hostile, and a scattering of immediately reopened accounts despite her noncommercial profile. Some important ex-customers looked up Wilson's boss to compliment him on his new Southwestern "complaints receiver."

This true story had several happy endings:

- Marcia became a star, eventually earning more money than most of her male counterparts.
- She became a popular speaker at Miller sales meetings, on various subtopics of living "on the give" instead of "on the take."
- She sensitized Miller and one-time chauvinists in other companies to the fact that there are plenty of other Marcias around, waiting to become stars in business if given the chance.

The story has two morals:

1. Living "on the give" beats the daily search for immediate gain.
2. Trade shows are a gold mine of growth opportunity for the energetic, the patient, and the imaginative future millionaires.

2. The Metamorphosis of a Forgettable Salesman into an Emerging Star at the Home Builders Show

This is another true story, but the name has been changed to protect the wealthy perpetrator.

Melvin Carter didn't fit the popular image of "star salesman." He was short, wore glasses, never drank or told ribald jokes, and found that people still didn't remember his name when he met them for the third time.

He determined that if he couldn't penetrate any major accounts during his third visit to the National Home Builders' Show, he would quit his job (with a heating/air conditioning supplier) and try another career.

The day before the show opened, Carter strolled around the Dallas Convention Center, curiously looking over countless exhibits. He came across a new trade association, devoted to upgrading construction standards in a category where cheap, substandard equipment was giving many new homes a "black eye."

Melvin sincerely liked the idea, and picked up a few dozen pieces of descriptive literature, plus copies of the new association's modest membership roster. During the next few days, he enthusiastically "talked up" the new association and distributed the material, giving it priority over his own company's commercial "pitch."

The approach worked wonders. Defense mechanisms went down. Doors opened. Business cards were exchanged. Before the show closed, several important prospects were calling him "Melvin." The new association gave him a pat on the back in its Show Newsletter. All this recognition boosted Carter's self-confidence. Before the next year's Builders' Show, he was a star with a healthy income, a promising career, and a "giving approach" to every business contact.

The two morals (repeated):

1. Living "on the give" is the more certain path to success.
2. Trade shows are a gold mine.

Perhaps the best true anecdote about Melvin Carter is still to be told, and it's a by-product of his commercial success.

Melvin was a lonely guy, haunting "singles parties" with little social success. One evening, sitting with an attractive female at still another singles party, he heard a comment he's heard before: "Melvin, you're really interesting, but I like taller men." Bolstered by his new career success, Melvin retorted: "But I'm a lot taller when I'm standing on all my bankbooks!"

A few months after they became intimate friends, the woman confessed that it wasn't the bankbooks that made the difference, but his spontaneous, witty response! Since this is a book about business and not psychology, we'll leave the reader to ponder her veracity!

3. The Organized "Ultimate Pro" Uses Seminars and Workshops for Back-Up

Richard McLeash was the well-prepared "ultimate professional" during his visits to the huge annual National Sporting

Goods Association trade show in Atlanta. His daily schedule consisted of early pre-show breakfasts with key clients, exhibit time and buyer appointments during show days, making the rounds of evening receptions, and organizing all the day's notes in his hotel room before "hitting the sack."

One day, when an important lunch date was canceled at the last moment, McLeash looked over the NSGA seminar program and immediately dropped in on a noon meeting entitled: "Boosting Athletic Team Business." McLeash knew instinctively that seminars are a great back-up for learning new ideas, and maybe meeting worthwhile new contacts.

The seminar speakers were dull, but McLeash noticed one obviously informed attendee whose remarks and questions from the audience were particularly pertinent. McLeash approached him after the meeting, exchanged business cards, and found a good, new friend in Philip Wendell.

Wendell was an ex-retailer who had recently purchased a marginal and relatively unknown manufacturing firm. He was vigorous, informed and ambitious, but lacked national contact and exposure.

McLeash unselfishly offered Wendell several routes to accelerated progress:

- A list of worthwhile regional shows
- An introduction to NSGA seminar program directors, so that Wendell could be considered as a moderator of future seminars
- Introductions to trade press editors, who were valuable sources of publicity for up-and-coming firms

Although manufacturers McLeash and Wendell never did business with each other, they became fast friends and mutual career assets.

McLeash later became VP Sales of his own firm, while Wendell prospered and became a major supplier in the sporting goods field. For many years, they exchanged valuable credit information, confidential performance data on sales reps, political gossip in the industry, research results, and sensitive inside ideas leading to informed decisions. The relationship was long lasting and mutually productive.

The two repeated morals:

1. Givers invariably receive.
2. Trade shows are a gold mine. Become a better miner. Every minute counts.

———————— ◇ ————————

GOOD GUYISM APPLIED: ADRIANE'S FUN FORMULA FOR CONVENTIONS AND EXPOS

If you read my bio at the back of this book you know that I'm a jack of many professional trades. That means I go to lots of different expos and conventions, each with a personality all its own. Meetings have included the American Booksellers Association, the American Bar Association, and the National Speakers Association, just to name a few.

But it was at the National Association of Radio Talk Show Hosts that I had the most fun, because I took along the prepublication text of this chapter to see if it would make a difference to me.

It did. Even the simplest suggestion—wear your badge—reminded me that I must make it easy for others to meet me. But more profound was the difference in attitude. Instead of envying the slick fellows with the big brochures, I found myself ready to give help and to listen to others. Every person at the booths or on the floor was an opportunity for "spotlight shining."

Frankly, it was much less exhausting to listen than to try breathlessly to "get my message across" in seconds. The aftermath was a pleasure, too. I came home knowing the favorite foods, tastes in furniture and other assorted needs, wants and desires of many participants. I learned *exactly* what they do for a living. As a result, I was better able to follow up with those I could help by giving them my business, my advice or other support.

Ultimately, there were fewer time-wasting sessions "barking up the wrong tree," explaining myself to the disinterested or preaching to the choir. Yes, I made better money-making contacts. And, yes, I will close more deals because I can target places where I am truly welcome.

SILENT SURVEY #7

Please answer these questions:

1. I have attended the following trade shows, conventions, etc., in the past 12 months: _____.

2. The most successful of them was _____.

3. The reason for the success was _____.

4. How can I duplicate the same success?
   Choose more carefully? _____
   Repeat my behavior? _____
   Seek out certain persons? _____
   Other _____

5. Going down the Good Guy suggestion list, did you follow the suggestions? _____
   If so, did it strengthen the event for you? _____
   If not, what can you improve on next time? _____

TO DO

Here are six new things I can do next time as participant or exhibitor that will make a difference:

1. _____
2. _____

3. _____

4. _____

5. _____

6. _____

How Good Guyism Combats Face-to-Face Shyness at Conventions

At a convention, expo or even an office party, has a well-meaning friend ever whispered these words in your ear?: "See that individual over there? You really ought to meet him (or her). It can make your career."

If you're like most Good Guys, that's enough to make you panic. How will you meet? Will you be rejected? Will the person *make* your career?

What's the problem here? Clearly, you are on the take and nothing but on the take. And I guarantee that, even if you get up the courage to say hello, it will get you nowhere. In fact, it may blow a real opportunity to meet the person later on.

And why are you, a big shot in your own sphere, all of a sudden tongue-tied? Simple, you are playing on another's turf.

There is one way to change the situation, fast. Shine the spotlight on the "career maker." What does he or she need? A fresh drink? A method of getting away from a boring conversationalist? A shopping bag to carry the paraphernalia from all the booths? Or does the person honestly need to be left alone to recover from all the on-the-takes who have moved in?

If the last is your conclusion, stay away. You'll live to be impressive another day.

CHAPTER 8

$$\Diamond$$

Influencing Unreachable People with the Power of Newsletters

How To Influence Powerful and Otherwise Unreachable People by Putting the Effective Pull of Newsletters To Work

One of the most effective business tools a Good Guy in any field or profession can use is the simple newsletter. It's a great door opener to business friendships and wealth.

A newsletter costs less than any other form of advertising or promotion but, when used correctly, it has much greater impact on customers, clients, and future target prospects. Anyone can use a newsletter: Manufacturers, service firms, nonprofit institutions, individual professionals . . . even political candidates!

Why is a newsletter so useful? The constituency of influentials and decision makers in your field or any other changes by 22 percent to 26 percent a year. In view of this instant change, you can't bet your future and your growth on last year's friends or customers. The newsletter helps you find, assist and influence existing clients and important new prospects . . . *but only if they perceive your newsletter as being "on the give" and free of hard sell.*

Later on in this chapter, please study the sample newsletter which Milt devised for a relatively unknown political candidate named George Pataki early in 1994, when Pataki was just beginning to seek his party's nomination to oppose the powerful three-time governor of New York State, Mario Cuomo. It followed all the rules Milt has used repeatedly and effectively.

While Milt doesn't claim the newsletter as a major factor in the exceptional campaign waged by Governor Pataki (elected in November 1994), it certainly must have helped. In any event, we wish this book's readers the same success Petaki enjoyed. Here are the guidelines for effective newsletters that achieve results:

1. A newsletter should have a positive name and a descriptive subtitle, both of which stress news, benefits, and some mention of the name of your firm or professional practice.
   Example:

   CARTER'S LITTLE PROFIT MAKERS
   Ideas, Info and Tips from Your Helpful Supplier

2. Continuity is vital. Readers must perceive the newsletter as an informative friend who visits them often. The ideal frequency is once a month, to stay fresh and newsy. The minimum is six times a year. If distributed only quarterly, newsletters become stale and less appealing.

3. Content is more vital than appearance. Your readers want information, help, and ideas. Too much color and fancy layout make the newsletter look like expensive advertising, to which many recipients have built up a "defense mechanism."

4. There should be many brief items on each page, as opposed to lengthy stories that overwhelm readers. You are "going fishing" for readers; more stories drop more hooks into the water.

5. Recognize the difference between headlines and titles, and use only headlines. A headline summarizes a con-

clusion or benefit, or a danger; it contains numbers or names, and usually has a verb. Titles are death to readership. Examples of bad titles:

Message from the President
Summary of Board Meeting
News from the Convention

6. The editor or writer of the newsletter should be on daily alert for material to create the upcoming issue. Every business day, the editor should have a handy envelope entitled "newsletter." Ideas, suggestions, news clippings, news developments, etc., should be inserted into the envelope constantly. When deadline time comes, there should be a selection process, not a searching process.

7. Once written, the newsletter should be produced and mailed quickly. An advance monthly production schedule should be known to all, and enforced seriously. Don't allow excessive color, layout, or executive approval to delay the newsletter. Today's fresh news becomes history if delayed for weeks.

8. Insert at least one response-stimulator in each issue. If anyone takes action after receiving your newsletter, it brings him or her closer to your company forever. Offer readers a new research study, a free reprint, or the opportunity to place colleagues' names on your free mailing list. As an example, see the bottom of page three of the Pataki September 1994 newsletter, which is reproduced in this chapter.

9. Keep your mailing list fresh and complete. This job is unglamorous but essential. Outdated names on the mailing list make a bad impression on readers. For culling the names, use Post Office returns, free offers in the newsletter itself, constant internal reminders to your staff, and a once-a-month personal physical examination of the mailing list.

Milt's Recommended Contents of an Effective Newsletter

- Calendar of important future events
- Separate news item on particularly important forthcoming major event
- Evidence of success of one of your products or services
- Customer experience testimonial (get customer permission first)
- Informative or newsworthy messages from your executives, provided that they lead off with a newsy headline and have legitimate news value
- Helpful business ideas gleaned and summarized from other sources, on such subjects as taxes, government regulation, money, labor, or other high-interest topics
- Warning about pitfalls, dangers, scams, and potential bad news in your industry
- Reminder about free, unusual, or extra service from your firm, which may not be known to all clients
- Offer to put other names of important activists on your free mailing list
- Use of numbers, statistics, or studies in the text and headlines that enhance credibility of the entire newsletter
- Evidence of the success or growth of your firm, but always devoid of "hard sell." The world out there loves to "ride with the winners," but it also likes to make that decision independently, rather than being directly solicited

This Pataki Newsletter Contained All the Vital Recommended Elements

Early in 1994, a virtually unknown New York State senator challenged three-term incumbent Governor Mario Cuomo, who was so strong that he was often mentioned as a United States presidential candidate. Cuomo was by far the better-known candidate, running for fourth term as Governor of New York.

Candidate George Pataki and his staff approved Milt's proposal to create a newsletter, directed to a statewide group of influentials. The mailing list consisted of candidates for local office and their campaign teams; demographic and geographic leaders throughout the state; major actual and prospective campaign contributors; the media; and other identifiable activists who could influence voter groups.

The newsletter aimed to create recognition and confidence in Senator Pataki among these VIPs. Milt suggested the positive newsletter title of *Winning with Pataki,* and the subtitle "Info and Ideas for Influentials, from New York's Next Governor." (Fortunately, that prophetic underline came true.)

Each monthly newsletter consisted of four pages (which is ideal), and was in black-and-white with no fancy layouts and no other color. Simplicity attracts readership.

Each newsletter contained a series of brief, helpful, and informative ideas on every page, intended to deliver information and useful ideas to the recipient. These readers would then recognize Pataki as a friend, source of help, and a "Good Guy."

Nothing in the series of newsletters directly requested financial contribution to the campaign. However, the evidence of progress plus the many positive reports were clear assets to a relatively lesser-known candidate's raising the funds necessary for a major campaign, while inspiring confidence and stronger backing as well.

Examine the pages of the Pataki newsletter. Notice the variety of good news, the verbs in each headline, the brevity and easy readership of each item, the frequent use of the word "free," the coming events, and the stimulus to respond. All of these are elements of effective newsletters that you can use and adapt for your own field or profession. Good luck.

WINNING WITH PATAKI

INFO & IDEAS FOR INFLUENTIALS, FROM NEW YORK'S NEXT GOVERNOR
© September 1994

THE BALL'S IN YOUR COURT, MARIO

On Friday, August 15th and Saturday, August 16th, the Pataki campaign allowed the press to inspect 15 years of tax returns and other records pertaining to the Senator's financial holdings and medical records. Now the onus is clearly on Cuomo, who has received hundred of thousands of dollars in speaking fees, to disclose his net worth.

INDEPENDENT LINE ADDED

In addition to running on the Republican and Conservative lines, Senator Pataki's name also will appear on the "Tax Cuts Now" line in the November election. Thanks to the efforts of the dedicated volunteers statewide, the campaign collected 54,453 signatures (only 15,000 are needed to qualify). This new line will allow voters who don't traditionally vote along major party lines to cast their ballots for Senator Pataki and Betsy McCaughey.

PATAKI OUT-RAISES CUOMO

During the most recent campaign finance period, the Pataki campaign far out-paced the Cuomo campaign in fund-raising. Senator Pataki raised over $1.8 million to Cuomo's $471, 289. While these results are encouraging, we still need to continue to raise substantial dollars to meet our $12 million goal -- a fund-raising level that will ensure victory in November.

Ambassador Charles Gargano, the campaign Finance Chairman, said "Once again, the fund-raising efforts of the Pataki/McCaughey campaign show that New Yorkers are rallying behind Senator Pataki. Donations continue to come in from all across the state from New Yorkers who recognize that in order to change Mario Cuomo's failed policies, we must elect George Pataki."

CUOMO EXCESSES EXPOSED

A "Top Ten List" of Mario Cuomo's Most Wasteful Spending was the subject of a press conference recently held in the New York City headquarters. Senator Pataki, accompanied by his faithful dog, Jefferson (named after the 3rd President), blasted Cuomo for wasting taxpayer dollars while not thinking twice about raising taxes.

The Top Ten List:
10. Out of State Christmas Trees

9. Taxpayer Funded Wedding Reception

8. Mansion Remodeling

7. $19,000 Stereo

6. Magazine subscriptions

5. $1,700 Grocery Bill

4. Daily Shoe Shines and Dry Cleaning

3. $484,000 for Maids / Chef / Mansion

2. "Air-Cuomo"

1. "Wee-Wee" Pads and Flea Collars

Senator Pataki vowed to cut the $484,000 mansion budget in half, and to use newspaper (he didn't say which daily) to meet Jefferson's needs.

PATAKI WINS BIG IN STRAW POLL

In a mock election conducted by the Farm Bureau of New York, George Pataki crushed Mario Cuomo by taking more than 90 percent of all the votes cast. Over 1,500 farmers from across the state cast their ballot as part of the Empire Farm Days which was held in Seneca Falls. Pataki collected 1,147 votes in comparison with 113 votes for Cuomo.

SEPT. 29TH FUND-RAISER SLATED

The next major fund-raiser is scheduled for September 29th at the New York Sheraton in New York City. If you are interested in being a Co-Chair or Vice-Chair, for this exciting event, contact the Finance Office ASAP -- these positions are filling fast.

NEW YORK CONTINUES TO LEAD... IN ALL THE WRONG AREAS

In Mario Cuomo's "New, New York", the Empire State remains the leader in the nation in woeful distinctions. Sadly, our record on crime, taxes, and job creation stands in stark contrast to other states which have been successful in taking back their streets and jump-starting their economies. The following facts and figures on crime and jobs/taxes support this assertation.

Crime

●The violent crime rate in New York State is 48 percent above the national average

●In New York State, a murder occurs every 3.7 hours, a rape occurs every 1.7 hours, an assault is perpetrated every six minutes, and a robbery / burglary is committed every 33 seconds.

●In the past decade, there have been more than 20,000 murders in New York State, yet Mario Cuomo continues to veto the death penalty despite its overwhelming support from New Yorkers.

Taxes/Jobs

●New York is second (only to Alaska) in combined state and local tax burden.

●During the national recession, New York lost 272,000 jobs, more than any other state.

●Since the beginning of the recovery, New York has lost 105,000 more jobs, while the rest of the nation gained almost 5.1 million jobs.

UPCOMING EVENTS IN SEPTEMBER

We have many events scheduled throughout the entire state for the month of September. If you are interested in attending an event in your area please contact the Finance Office at (212) 370-9494 to find out when Senator Pataki or Betsy McCaughey will attend an event in your area. Also call if you are interested in hosting an event at your home, office, or at a restaurant or club.

PEF DROPS CUOMO

Taking a cue from CSEA, the Public Employees Federation (PEF) -- the largest white-collar state workers union -- voted overwhelmingly not to endorse Mario Cuomo. The 57,000-member union took only 15 minutes to render its verdict after Cuomo asked for its backing at a meeting earlier this month. This is a serious blow to Cuomo's re-election bid.

The Albany Times-Union reported that "Failing to get the union's backing costs Cuomo not only votes and campaign contributions, but access to a sophisticated political operation that can send out literature, knock on doors, fill rallies and get out votes. Their support is particularly helpful upstate and on Long Island -- two areas where polls say the governor is in trouble."

PATAKI BOARDS GOP EXPRESS

In his continued effort to reach out to voters in every part of the state, Senator Pataki recently barnstormed throughout the Southern Tier and the Finger Lakes regions aboard Rep. Amo Houghton's GOP Express. Betsy McCaughey and Bernadette Castro also were on the campaign bus. The seven-county bus tour started in Jamestown, and before the day ended, Senator Pataki delivered his message to voters in Olean, Wellsville, Corning, Horseheads, Watkins Glen, and Auburn. Senator Pataki told his supporters "We've got to make this state No. 1 in economic opportunity instead of No. 1 in taxes and losing jobs. We still have the people, the competitive drive and the work ethic. All we need now are the people in Albany who will allow us to be No. 1 again in all the right categories."

FREE INTERNSHIPS AVAILABLE

Unlike other political internships, the Pataki for Governor campaign offers an exciting opportunity to gain first-hand knowledge and experience in such fields as politics, media, finance, and other areas -- all for free. If interested, please contact:

Montgomery Engel
Volunteer / Internship Coordinator
WINNING WITH PATAKI
360 Lexington Avenue - 7th Floor
New York, NY 10017

or call (212) 370-9494

DO YOU HAVE A GOOD CAMPAIGN ISSUE OR IDEA?

If you have an issue or idea that you think would be useful to the campaign, type your idea on a two-page memo and address it to:

> Director, Issues and Research
> WINNING WITH PATAKI
> 360 Lexington Avenue - 7th Floor
> New York, NY 10017

PATAKI PLANS TRIP TO SYRACUSE

On September 20th, Senator Pataki will be visiting Syracuse for a huge fund-raiser being held at the Hotel Syracuse. Tickets to the dinner are only $200 per person, and if you or a friend are interested in attending, please contact Paula O'Brien at (315) 471-2020.

PATAKI TO COME HOME ON SEPT. 28

Senator Pataki will visit his home turf for a rally and a dinner on September 28th in Cortland. If you or a friend are interested in attending please contact Jack Gaffney at (914) 737-1422

REMINDER: LETTER TO EDITOR CAN MAKE A DIFFERENCE

As the campaign heats up and Election Day draws near, letters to the editor of any daily or weekly newspaper become more popular, and receive more attention. We therefore repeat the reminder from an earlier newsletter that those letters yield attention, credibility, and votes for the Pataki ticket or any local candidate -- at no cost at all! For best results and chance of publication, follow these rules:

●Type double-spaced
●Send to only one newspaper
●Refer to an important topic or recent news report
●Add fresh, unreported, or relatively unknown facts
●Give an opinion or conclusion
●Recommend action by readers
●Sign your name (it will be printed) and give your phone number (it will not be printed, but may be used by the newspaper to verify your letter).

67 DAYS LEFT UNTIL VICTORY NIGHT!

From September 1st, there are only 67 days left until election night. That means we all have a lot of work to do. Here are some things you can do between now and then to ensure victory:

●Make sure you and all your friends and family members are registered to vote.
●If you are not going to be around on Election Day, be sure to vote by absentee ballot.
●Write a rolodex letter to all your friends and relatives, asking them to support Senator Pataki's campaign by voting, getting the message out, and by financially supporting the campaign.
●Write separate letters to the editors of all papers that you read.
●Serve on Senator Pataki's Finance Committee by calling his Finance Chairman, Ambassador Charles A. Gargano at (212) 370-9494.
●Request a bumper sticker and yard sign and place them on your car and in your home or store window.
●Volunteer at the Campaign headquarters or at your local headquarters.

We must make sure that we do everything possible between now and November 8th. We have only 67 days to roll up our sleeves and work hard for the future of New York State.

FREE HANDY "ISSUES" BOOKLET AVAILABLE TO CAMPAIGN ACTIVISTS

A handy little pocket guide to election issues, entitled "Issues '94," has been made available for use by candidates, teams, and campaign activists. It was printed by The Heritage Foundation, 214 Massachusetts Ave. N.E., Washington, D.C. 20002, phone (202) 546-4400.

A typical chapter on CRIME (pages 32-53) give details, issues, alternatives, etc., on the "tidal wave of crime" which has been victimizing millions of Americans each year. It contains statistics on prisons, parole, repeat offenders, social costs, early release programs, etc. and concludes with a most informative 14-point reform proposal.

There are also chapters and sections on welfare, budget, taxation, and congressional issues. We recommend the booklet to all interested in WINNING WITH PATAKI.

ZIP CODE 10017
PERMIT No.7404
NEW YORK, NY
PAID
U.S. POSTAGE
BULK RATE

New York, NY 10017
360 Lexington Avenue - 7th Floor
WINNING WITH PATAKI

INFLUENTIAL MAGAZINE SAYS IT'S CUOMO'S "TIME TO GO!"

A recent article in NEW YORK Magazine, which has the reputation of being informed, influential, and independent, asks "Is it Time for Cuomo To Go?" On the front cover, the magazine concludes "Mario Cuomo just might lose this election. And that might not be so bad." The article analyzes Cuomo's record in detail, and gives him high marks in rhetoric, but much lower grades in virtually all the serious issues surrounding his administration and the 1994 campaign.

Typical headlines on some of the continuing pages include "Cuomo has done little of value, or at least far less than he ought to have done"; "Cuomo's economic development; higher taxes and more regulations"; followed by detailed analysis of Cuomo's performance in the areas of economy, education, health, welfare, and crime.

For your own copy of the article, write to the Pataki Campaign Headquarters at 360 Lexington Avenue, New York, N.Y. 10017 or call (212) 370-9494.

YOU ARE INVITED TO PRIMARY NIGHT CELEBRATION

On Tuesday, September 13th the Pataki Campaign will host a Primary Celebration that you are invited to attend. The victory party will be at the New York Hilton and will begin at 8 p.m. Senator Pataki and Betsy McCaughey will be in attendance.

Don't forget to vote in the primary!!

DID YOU KNOW ABOUT... GEORGE PATAKI ?

George Pataki, while serving as Mayor of Peekskill, Assemblyman, and State Senator, accumulated a record of achievements. Here are a list of some of the awards he received, leadership positions he has held, and legislation he helped pass:

AWARDS
● New York Times State Legislative Honor Roll 1988
● "Friend of Small Business" 1992 from the National Federation of Independent Businesses
● "Friend of the Farmer Award" 1990 & 1991 from the New York State Farm Bureau
● "Empire State Vietnam Veterans Encampment Salute" 1989

LEADERSHIP
● Chairman, Senate Ethics Committee
● Former Ranking Republican, Assembly Education Committee
● Member, Senate Banking Committee
● Member, Senate Housing and Community Development Committee
● Former Member, Assembly Education Committee
● Former Member, Assembly Ways and Means Committee

LEGISLATIVE RECORD
● Sponsored Death Penalty for Certain Murders
● Sponsored Established Public Housing Drug Elimination Pilot Program
● Sponsored Stiffer Penalties for Possession of Cocaine or Crack
● Sponsored Expanded Senior Citizens Property tax Exemption
● Sponsored Established Landmark Child Support Guildlines Law

—————◇—————

GOOD GUYISM APPLIED:
ADRIANE'S SECRETS TO PUBLISHING
A NEWSLETTER FAST AND CHEAP

As a strong advocate of newsletter use, perhaps even more than Milt is, here are my seven magic bullets for getting it done fast and right:

1. Use PageMaker® or similar software; the desktop publishing is a breeze.

2. Visit your local college and interview students to do the layout and proofreading; they are dedicated and economical, and if you provide good training they will get credits for their work.

3. When you sit down to write, ask "What would my reader want to know?" Never write about what you like, no matter how much fun, unless your audience would be interested, too.

4. Never buy "canned" newsletters from a turnkey operation. You get them with your financial statements every month. Do you ever read them? Write the copy yourself.

5. Use the best value print shop you can find. (See guideline #10 in Chapter 1: Never buy the "cheapest.") I have found this to be an industry where quality, service and price do not always correlate. If you are on a shoestring, use a print shop or photocopy machine.

6. Make your image consistent. If the letter is homey, address envelopes by hand (I started with only 20 readers). After 200, I went Hollywood!

7. And, most important of all, ask your readers to send articles, tips, ideas, etc. If you are in sales, it's the best door opener I have seen. If you want to reach someone who is hard to get to, write his or her profile for the

newsletter. You can interview the person, do research and open the door to friendship. The business will follow.

SILENT SURVEY #8

Please answer these questions:

1. Who should receive my newsletter?
2. How will it benefit them?
3. How often can I get one out? (Be realistic.)
4. Who in the office could write it?
5. Can I afford a freelance writer? (Call the American Society of Journalists and Authors to get prices; also contact your local college for student writers.)

TO DO

Pick an occasion—Election Day, if need be. Analyze it with a one-time newsletter. After you get some experience, keep going.

CHAPTER 9

◇

Converting Complaints to New Business, More Sales and Long-Term Alliances

Handling Complaints Is the Good Guys' Secret Weapon for Business, Loyalty, Reputation, and Creating Wealth

About a year after Gralla Publications had acquired *National Jeweler* Magazine (a trade publication then running dead last in its field), I got an angry call from a leading manufacturer of wedding rings.

The call reached me, as publisher, because the editorial staff was worn out by this man's previous periodic bitter calls. The staff had secretly identified him as "Mister Complaint."

This man never gave the improving magazine a compliment or a share of his advertising budget, and he was known to be bad-mouthing Gralla Publications to others influential in the jewelry industry.

This time he had two new complaints: Alleged disrespect by one of the magazine writers, and alleged lack of adequate publicity in an important story preceding the national jewelry show.

I thanked him for calling personally; asked him to slow down so that I could take notes; turned off my defensive ego; and turned on the formula that follows in this chapter.

The results were so immediate and positive that I use this enriching experience as a case history in seminars (to my own staff and to other business groups) on the absolute theory that "You Can Get Rich Handling Complaints."

I won't identify "Mister Complaint" for you because he's still my strong personal friend. But after the door first opened, he became a positive news source, a loyal advertiser, and an advocate of *National Jeweler* Magazine to others in the jewelry industry.

It can happen to you! Read this chapter, rehearse the formula, look over your own shoulder the next time a noisy complainer comes your way, and take another step on your own road to wealth!

In our society, complaints are a way of life. We can treat them either as disruptive, or as a golden opportunity for new prospects, reputation, friendships, and business growth.

People complain about products, services and what we did or neglected. They complain by phone, in person and via third party "messengers." It's a way of life in our society. We can treat complaints as disruptive or as a door-opening opportunity for enhanced reputation and business growth.

Good guys start off with this attitude:

1. On a scale of 1 to 10, most of our average daily business contacts give us an attention rating of "3" or "5." The complainer is giving us a rare perfect gift of the attention level of "10."

2. *Complainers want attention now!* Deny it, and their future anger will kill you. Deliver it, and you have an ally for life.

Before we outline the essential and highly profitable steps in handling complaints, we want to list some serious but common complaint-handling errors:

- "You are speaking to the wrong person."
- "You are always complaining."

- "You are dead wrong."
- "I'm too busy right now."
- "This is no big deal."
- "Everybody is complaining about that."

Here are the more appropriate steps that will work 99 percent of the time in diffusing complaints. The steps will also create from each complaint a loyal, solid and permanent ally who will give you business and tell the world about you positively.

1. Thank the complainer. He or she is absolutely helping you in your business. Your sincere thanks will diffuse at least some of the anger.

2. Ask if it is OK to take notes. Nobody ever tells you not to take notes. It assures the complainer you are responding with serious attention.

3. Repeat the complainer's name a couple of times, particularly if you have had limited contact in the past. This signals even more personal attention.

4. After hearing the first complaint, ask if the complainer is angry about anything else. Sometimes the complaining party is concealing anger over a previous unrelated event. Find this out immediately.

5. Ask if anyone else is involved. Sometimes complainers are just "messengers" for someone higher up. This question helps you identify and respond to others who may be involved.

6. Read back your notes to the complainer. This will convince him or her again of your serious attention.

7. Ask the complainer what he or she believes should be done. This transfers the discussion to the future, whereas the real or imaginary injustice is in the past. The complainer must now consider and verbalize what is wanted. He may still be angry and unrealistic. Let's assume that he demands items A, B, C, and D.

Make notes, but don't decide or answer immediately. Repeat the demands to show you heard it all.

8. Promise to investigate promptly and resolve the problem by a certain agreed-upon deadline. Your promised investigation will give the complainer and his allies some chance to cool off.

9. Begin using the "uphill syndrome." The higher up in your organization the complainer reaches, the more he is satisfied with the attention he is getting. Managers, executives, and owners should be made aware of the complaint and the proposed resolution.

10. Before the deadline, give the complainer "intermediate attention."

    Example: If you promised an answer by noon Friday, call or write Wednesday afternoon to assure the complainer that the investigation is continuing, and that a reply will be forthcoming.

11. Don't miss the deadline! Regardless of your other efforts, if you have promised an answer and resolution by noon Friday, and have not called by 2 PM Friday, the anger will be compounded. If you can't answer by the deadline, make an explanatory call and ask for a brief postponement.

12. Never say "no" to the complainer. Let's assume he has asked for A, B, C, and D. Three of these are possible, but item "C" is either impossible, too expensive, or both. Call and offer him A, B, D, and "E," which is something you are throwing in he didn't even ask for. Forget about "C." He will probably forget about it as well. If he does still demand "C," stick to your guns.

13. You can't please everybody in the world unless you want to give away the store. Sooner or later, you'll meet a complainer who just will not be satisfied. You can do business profitably without him.

Cherish Our Complaint Rights— They're a Symbol of Freedom

In my first visit to Russia in 1971, I was astounded not only by the dreadful living conditions of the people, but also by their total and uncomplaining acceptance of their lifestyle.

Their dwelling places were rationed to a sparse few square meters; they waited in long lines for many basic consumer products and services; and party committees made important decisions concerning their jobs, education, travel, vacations and other matters.

The most amazing part of this process (which, of course, has since disappeared) was that, in more than a week in Moscow and other major cities, not one person was heard to complain. I recall concluding that, in the United States and the rest of the free world, we should appreciate fully the freedom symbolized by the right to complain, as well as the free exercise of that right.

And in the business world particularly, the rich Good Guys have learned that each complaint is a potential open door to new friendships, new success and new wealth!

True-Life Adventures in Complaint Handling . . . Score Two Wins, One Loss, Many Useful Lessons!!

Complaint #1

An important kitchen cabinet manufacturer, celebrating its 25th anniversary, offered the editor of *Kitchen Business* (a Gralla Publication) a completed story on the company's history. The editor declined to publish it, on the basis of reader-interest standards. The company complained, stating that (a) a public relations firm had prepared the story at great cost, and (b) it threatened to cancel its lucrative advertising contract unless the magazine complied.

Solution:

A higher executive of the magazine gave the manufacturer this suggestion: "Let us interview your top executive, who's been there all 25 years. The subject will be 'The best 25 business lessons we learned in 25 years.' You'll get more real reader attention and respect. We'll continue the reader-interest standards that you and other advertisers value."

Outcome:

The company liked the idea, gave the interview, then reprinted the article for mail use during the 25th anniversary year. The advertising contract was stronger than ever.

Lessons:

1. Use the "uphill syndrome" (response to complaint came from a higher executive).
2. Introduce an alternative "Yes" to avoid the "No" to an impossible complainer demand.

Complaint #2

An advertising agency accused a magazine's production manager of using the wrong ad in a recent issue. The production manager argued defensively. The client advertiser then called personally, and the production manager argued some more.

Solution:

None

Outcome:

Advertiser account lost for two years

Lessons:

1. School *all* employees in complaint handling, including "listen but don't argue" rule.
2. Notify higher executive before irreparable damage is done.

Complaint #3

An advertising manager notified our magazine's regional representative that the annual ad contract is not being renewed because "You've been goofing up some of our listings in your annual Directory."

Solution:

Representative listens, takes notes, asks questions. Two questions in the sequence yield information:

1. Is anyone else involved? "Yes, my boss, VP of Sales, Bill Halloran."
2. Are you angry about anything else? "You better ask Halloran."

Halloran is approached by the magazine's top executive and is pleased with the attention. He has cut his ad budget, so two other magazines are "in," and we are "out." He was really angry with us for "not attending my press conference." However, we find that two of our editors did indeed attend the event. Halloran tells the publisher his decision was uninformed and arbitrary.

Outcome:

We got the ad program back. A less enterprising magazine is "out." Halloran is impressed with three of our people. We discover for the first time that the ad manager is a "front" for Halloran, who really calls the shots.

Lessons:

1. Always ask if anyone else is involved. You may have received the original complaint from a "messenger."

2. Always ask about any other complaints. The first one may not be the real problem.

3. Use the "uphill syndrome" when needed. The Hallorans of the world are more impressed by the boss than by his minions, even when the reply is the same.

———————— ◇ ————————

GOOD GUYISM APPLIED: HOW ADRIANE WENT FROM A GUILT-RIDDEN COMPLAINT EVADER TO A RESPECTED AND RICHER COMPLAINT HANDLER

I was a guilty complaint handler, so concerned with not being loved that I treated every complaint as a mortal threat to my self-esteem. The results were a lot of dodged phone calls, butterflies in the stomach and increasingly angry clients. Then I learned the 13-step Good Guy formula. Here's what happened many years ago when I first tested it.

A radio sponsor was upset that I had advertised a financial seminar in the same location where he had held one for years, and within only a few days of his. The radio station would have lost a great customer and, perhaps, I would have lost my job if he could not be satisfied.

The trouble was that the seminar in conflict with his was sponsored by another cherished advertiser who had a signed contract from me and had already paid my fee. Of course, my complaining sponsor insisted that I cancel my seminar (with 400 people already having purchased tickets).

I listened, took notes, read back his request, and told him I would get back to him in two days. I did, with a great new idea. I would not cancel my seminar or move it elsewhere, but I would appear for no fee at his event. I would design a different topic, and even give his audience the scoop on my latest book by providing some free copies as door prizes. He was so happy that he booked me for four seminars and has become one of my staunchest supporters.

I know that these perfect endings seem too good to be true, but they really happen. And they happen all the time if you genuinely want to help, not just protect yourself or get rid of the nuisance posed by the next "Mister Complaint."

Danielle, Adriane's Secretary, Faces a Real Tough Customer

This morning, I received a phone call from the husband of one of Adriane's faithful listeners and a newsletter subscriber. He was calling me to say "It is now April; March has come and gone," and his wife, who had subscribed to the newsletter back in November, had not received it. I explained to this gentleman, as I had to other subscribers, that bulk mail was too slow, that Adriane would never mail that way again and that I would personally mail out a copy of the newsletter that day.

This gentleman became very angry and annoyed, not only about everything that had transpired but directly with me. He got extremely nasty, impatient and very obnoxious. I tried to re-explain it to him and apologize for any inconvenience, but he did not want to listen to reason. The way in which I really wanted to answer was impolite, so I held in my feelings and just stayed upset. I was very angry and disturbed that this person was going to "kill the messenger." He hung up on me.

I reviewed Milt's 13 steps to handling a complainer and called him back. Was I unhappy! This is the person who had just set my whole day off the wrong way. For the life of me I did not want to have anything to do with this individual again.

I took a deep breath and put what little smile that was left back on my face and announced myself and where I was calling from. I thanked him for calling us with his complaints and advised him once again of the situation, this time reversing the order of the 13 steps. To my surprise, he became human! He was very kind, understanding and even thankful that I was trying to help him. This did not sound like the same inconsiderate person I had spoken with earlier in the day. Oddly enough, I said nothing new. It seems that the order in which I spoke made the difference. Thanking him first, asking to write things down, suggesting I talk to his wife to explain to her as well, etc.

SILENT SURVEY #9

Please answer the following questions:

1. How do I handle complaints—ignore, give in, pass along to staff?
2. Do complaints worry me, make me anxious?
3. Have I trained my staff in the 13-point method? If not when will I?
4. What kind of complainer am I? Timid, loud, insistent?
5. How do I feel when my requests and demands are met? When they are not met?

TO DO

- Create a 13-step list that you keep by the telephone. Use it for complaints.
- Start a complaint record file. Note the date, nature, source of the complaint and what you promised to do. Do it.
- Note the immediate result of your action. Note the result three months later: Is the client/customer still yours? Did you lose him/her? What went right? What went wrong?

By now you may be exhausted trying to be a Good Guy. There are lots of new things to do—mostly detailed work. But help is on the way. Read on. . . .

◇

CHAPTER 10

Building Your Business Using Adriane's Good Guy Telephone Do's and Don'ts

How To Avoid Telephone Turn-Off with Good Guy Etiquette

The basic Good Guy formula should infuse every step you make in business. As much as 40 percent of your work time may be spent on the telephone. If you are salesperson, it may be as high as 80 percent. It is critical to talk the Good Guy talk.

Before you pick up the telephone, ask yourself: "How will my call help the listener?" Do that, and every call will be another step to success. In Chapter 9, you read about calls that come to you to present complaints. But, for now, let's look at a call that you make to complain.

Ordinarily, you want to scream and yell. You are angry. You want something for yourself. So how can you *help* the other guy?

Are you about to stop doing business with the firm? Refuse to pay? Take other detrimental action? A Good Guy provides a chance to save the situation.

See the difference in these opening lines:

- "This is the second time you misprinted my newsletter. I demand that you send me a second printing free. You're the worst printers I ever dealt with."

- "I just calculated that I spend about $3,000 a month in printing. I can't send out misprinted material, and this is the second example from your shop. If you want to work with me, I'll need an immediate corrected second printing free of charge."

Maybe you want to touch base, get business, make an appointment. There is no situation where you cannot turn your call into a Good Guy gesture. In fact, all you have to do is verbally follow Milt's letter-writing strategy.

Here's an example in the toughest telephone arena in the world—the cold call.

"Hello, Mrs. Sims. This is John Branch from Detroit Universal Life. After doing a major study on the contribution of homemakers, we found that it would cost $40,000 a year to replace their services. The study is a real eye-opener and fun to read. I'll send it to your office or home, whichever is better for you. We really want to educate folks about how family finances are affected by the loss of the homemaker."

The Premise Is That Outgoing Calls Must Be Made To Extend Help, Not To Be on the Take

When you make a call to someone you know, the Good Guy philosophy can make a big difference in business results and tangible success. To begin with, because you are a recognized Good Guy, people will take your call. You will very rarely be put off. Even those who know you only by reputation feel good vibrations instead of resistance when you call.

Further, most of your calls will be to do something for them, keep a promise you made, give them information. They are the takers, you are on the give. These are easy calls to make; you never get rejected.

But what if the situation requires you to make a request, get a response, have them take an action? Perhaps you want them to commit to a purchase. Here is the surprising Good Guy approach:

If it's critical—don't demand an answer on the phone. Don't set yourself up for "no" by expecting a decision on an important matter in a phone conversation that you initiated. If it is critical that action be taken, use the phone to set up a discussion meeting.

There's an old image of rich guys doing business on the golf course. That's symbolically true. The best deals are made in person, at work or at play, so don't expect too much from your phone. It should not be used for life and death business. That's best done in person and even through letters. The phone is to tidy up details.

Don't overestimate the telephone. To an attorney, it's like a pretrial deposition. You can lose a case on the deposition, but you can't win one. Same with the phone. You can close off communication, but it's rare that you'll make the sale, the arrangement or finalize the contract without putting pressure of an anti-Good Guy style on the person you are speaking with. So, don't try.

SILENT SURVEY #10

Please answer these questions:

1. What type of calls do you usually make? Routine appointment? Sales? Negotiation? Complaint? Customer service?

2. How many calls do you make a day?

3. What do you want to *accomplish* with these calls?

4. Do you make them yourself or are they made by staff?

5. Do you prioritize your calls by importance and frequency?

As with letters, determine a strategy for each type of call, concentrating on the important ones more. Pass off the frequent, more routine ones to staff, providing them with Good Guy training to handle them (see Chapter 3).

Telephone Etiquette and the Terrors of "Please Hold"

The telephone is *America's number one business building and sustaining power tool.* Yet, only recently has any thought been given to its best and proper use. Writing about Good Guy telephone etiquette would seem trivial, except that the incidence of angering, annoying and even losing clients and influential associates with Bad Guy telephone habits is widespread. It's nonsensical to wage a sales campaign, get the response call you seek and have your prospective client hear the word "hold" even before either party has said "hello." Here are the daily habits that will keep both you and your entire office Good Guys while on the phone.

For Both Incoming and Outgoing Calls Take Notes and Be Sure the Other Guy Knows It

Look at your desk and the desks of your secretary, receptionist, and telemarketer—everyone who represents your business on the phone.

Is there a simple telephone note pad with enough room to take really good messages from the person being spoken with? You need to show him or her that someone is really listening; that's your number-one goal. Your number-one method of reaching that goal is to clearly say, "For follow-up purposes, I'm taking notes." Then take them.

At the very least, the notes should reflect the name, telephone number and best times to return the call. (Make sure that all information is retrieved each time there is a phone contact.)

But your notes should also contain ideas for what you can do for the person on the phone. You'll need that for your Good Guy style follow-up. Think in terms of Chapter 6 on letters. What do you need to remember about the conversation to fill in the blanks in your Good Guy letter? That's what every telephone conversation should yield—one or more things you can do for the caller.

A Reminder: Let the person know you are paying attention by mentioning the notes you are taking.

Good Guy Phone Pad

Name of Caller:

Date:

Time:

Best Time to Call Back:

Best Place to Reach Caller:

Alternative Place:

Purpose of Call:

Promises Made:

Notes for Future GG Efforts:

Time-Sensitive Action That Must Be Taken:

Smile When You Talk on the Phone: It's an Attitude, Not a Lip Position

What do you see while you are talking on the phone? Look in the cubby, or on the wall, or on you drinking cup. Is there a nasty slogan? You know what I mean: a drinking cup, a notepad, a sign, a paperweight with one of the popular "bumper sticker"–style slogans that are just plain mean-spirited. "Your problem is obvious," with a photo of a person with his you-know-what up his you-know-where. Or how about "I owe, I owe, so off to work I go"? Cute, huh? So what's so bad about these slogans and what do *they* have to do with the telephone?

Everyone, from tyrants to the folks on Madison Avenue, understands the power of subliminal suggestion. If you are on the telephone and you are staring at a symbol of anger and resistance toward work, what tone of voice do you expect to convey? What emotional image comes through? The worst, whether you intend it or not.

All telephone conversation is a matter of signals, electronic sound and human emotion, and most offices are chaotic enough, especially for the receptionist—who is your first ambassador and line of defense. Don't arm him, her or yourself with negative tools.

Incoming Calls Must Make the Caller Believe in the Efficiency of Your Office and Your Willingness to Help: Say "Hello," Not "Hold"—Not Even "Please Hold!"

Every call should start with a "hello," and the name of your firm stated clearly. Then follow with "How can I help you?"

After that, listen. Do not put the caller on hold!

If you or whoever is answering *must* put the person on hold, say so first, and offer a choice of calling back. Lately, even automated answering machines are not only apologizing for the hold and playing music (a semi-good idea to be discussed below), but also coming back on the line to report how many minutes are left before a live person can take the call.

You should provide the same attention.

Have your receptionist, secretary or assistant ask whether the person can wait, explain for how long, and then, if there is a "yes I'll hold" response, press the hold button.

Get back to the caller as soon as possible. If you do not you have probably lost the business or other benefit of the call: Plain and simple.

I have heard a secretary say, "I can't get any work done around here; the phone keeps ringing!" Answering calls *is* the work! Make sure your whole office knows that—even the boss. Point out telephone answering improvements that can work beyond your own desk.

Anyone Who Answers Is Responsible To Help: If You Are Not Ready To Help, Don't Answer the Phone

Many times the person who answers passes the caller on to the next person, and an endless chain of useless encounters ensues. The bigger the company the more this happens. The solution to this problem actually was discussed in Chapter 3 on getting more help from your help. Everyone who answers the phone must know who is qualified to provide specific assistance. Everyone must sound authoritative and take pride in providing help or directing the person to the correct source. Many people are so happy to "get rid" of a caller that the prospect of sending him or her to another department is obvious in their gleeful tone. How do you make your employees concerned with helping? Reward them for good work and train them (and yourself) in telephone skills:

- Ask, "Can I Help?" Always say "Help" even if it's only to get the caller to the correct person.
- Take complete messages and note the best time to call back if no one can help at the moment.
- If the caller rambles, shorten the conversation by asking again for the exact help required. See Chapter 9 on complaints to get an overview on speaking to angry people. Make sure you know what people really want or you probably can't help them.
- If it's going to take a while to get back to the caller, offer to call back or explain how long he or she will be on hold.
- If the caller is angry, or perhaps even rude or fresh, offer to help by taking notes. "I can hear that you are very up-

set. Let me take down your message so we can straighten this out for you once and for all."

How Two Potential Good Guys Can Ruin Their Business by "Giving Bad Phone"

I met two young architects, hungry for business, at a home-improvement fair. A good potential client, I called, and, as expected, the industrious duo were working late. Here's what happened:

"Hello." That is the greeting, so I ask, "Is this A&B Architects?" The answer comes, "Well, this is Sammy." "Yes, but is this an architectural firm?" "Yes, but I have to get them." The phone is put down and one of the principals picks it up. I mention the home-improvement show and explain my interest in an addition to a Victorian house. I also comment that their brochure says they won an award and that an article was published in a journal about their work. I tell the architect that I have called my local library for a copy of the publication, without success. He acknowledges the article, and offers me two hours of free time at my own home (they are several miles away). I explain that I am going to Europe and will call when I return to take him up on his offer. He says thanks and goodby. When I return months later, I still have not received anything in writing.

These young men *want* business. I watched them at the home show, with an expensive booth and plenty of free, also expensive, giveaways. However, very few people showed up, and they looked glum. As for my call, I love my house and would like to expand—perfect business for them. Let us count the ways they goofed by phone:

1. The architects' helper is totally untrained in answering the phone.

2. Their helper is totally without interest in whether I become a client or not.

3. They missed the Good Guy opportunity to mail a copy of their article to me.

4. Worst of all: They never asked for or got my name, address or telephone number. If I don't make another call they will always wonder, "Who was that lady who wanted the addition?"

What did A&B Architects offer? Hard work, talent, free time. So, the guys will let me waste hours of their time, but they won't take two minutes to make a serious professional connection on the telephone. Why? Because they are too busy *working* to be a success!

The telephone is the gateway to your business. Don't close it because you're working too hard to pay attention.

The Pros and Cons of Music and Electronics

- Many telephone strategies are a matter of taste. Music on hold—I prefer information to music while I'm waiting. My favorite is information about the company I am calling—like a newsletter on the telephone.

- Speakerphones—I dislike speakerphones intensely, while others think they are great. Make your own survey. If you use a speakerphone, don't start with it on. *Start with it off, and ask if it's OK with the other guy.* Choose "hold" filler for its soothing or informational content, or both.

- Voice mail—Apply Good Guy common sense to your voice mail system. Make sure that a caller can reach a live person in an emergency. State if you are out of town and won't be able to answer shortly; ask enough questions to determine the name, address and a good time to call back. Be convincing that you are really sorry you missed the call.

SILENT SURVEY #11

Be your own telephone consultant:

How many calls do you make and receive a day? Which individuals answer in your office? How do they say hello? What is their attitude? Is it their main job or a subordinate job? Have you trained them in phone handling? Do they have a script that would help in making or answering calls? If not, write one.

Hold a telephone-use session. You can get video training for your office from The Telephone Doctor (30 Hollenberg Ct., St. Louis, MO 63044; 314-291-1012; fax: 314-291-3710).

In reviewing Chapter 3 on training and office by-laws, make telephone treatment a priority.

CHAPTER 11

◇

Using High-Tech Tools
To Get Speedy Results

The Automated Good Guy
Gets Results Using High-Tech Tools
and the Information Superhighway

As you review the many components that make up the Good
Guy style, you may feel overwhelmed with the "extra" work
needed to say thanks, to be ever punctual, to create appropriate
letters and more.

A teacher of Milt's once said, "The reward for good work is
more work." As a corollary, those of you dedicated to success,
most likely, already have too much to do.

However, consider this: The Good Guy method helps everyone work smarter, not harder. Especially in the chapters on improving the amount and quality of help you can get from others,
you learned to lighten your load and direct energy to the things
that get you where you want to go.

Even so, the prospect of writing more letters, answering
more calls and more complaints may seem daunting. Luckily,
we have technology that can make us *automated* Good Guys.

There are endless varieties of cellular phones, beeper systems
and answering devices that make you more responsive to the
needs of others. Use them along with any other hardware that

can make you faster, more comprehensive and more efficient in delivering what you promise. Of course, the quintessential piece of Good Guy hardware is the fax. *What required a first-class stamp and three days for delivery in the past is accomplished in only a few seconds today.* You can send your letters, fax an article of use to the recipient or fulfill a promise to a complainer in a snap.

But to really be an automated Good Guy you must integrate new products and technology into your everyday work system, and it isn't easy for some of us. As much as we may want to fight it, the future is now, and it is essential to make the new technology our friend.

Even if you are a sole proprietor, go kicking and screaming if you must, but get a computer that works with state-of-the-art speed and the most current software. For example, a Good Guy uses a scanner to input newspaper articles and other documents directly into faxes and letters. A copier goes without saying, but the new portable copiers that add a pound to your laptop work well for people on the road who need to fulfill promises speedily.

Take a survey of your own office in terms of each item of equipment, its age, its usefulness, and the cost of an upgrade.

Hardware

With so much on the market, it will be easy to find the very products and services to implement a Good Guy system. In fact, we have too much choice. So, "picks" here are limited to items that specifically aid in pursuing the Good Guy methodology with vigor.

Software

Writing Good Guy Letters in a Hurry

- 401 Great Letters for Windows ($49.95 from Great Bear Technology 1-800-795-4325) includes business-to-business letters. It also features complaint letters for you to write to others that get results Good Guy style.

- ACT software produces specific salutations for every letter you send. Your correspondence never looks like a form letter. You can come up with a Good Guy idea of interest to hundreds of clients, customers and others, and send each a personal letter (Symantec Corp. 1-800-441-7234).

- 101 Sales and Marketing Letters includes collection letters, introductions to your business, and, of course, our cherished thank-you letters (Great Bear).

- Also by Great Bear, 808 Great Letters includes the entire Great Bear Library, including 101 Love Letters!

Telephoning the Good Guy Way

- Your PC can become a voice mail system with I'll Get It!, by Moon Valley Software. It can handle from 1 to 99 voice mail accounts, each with user-defined access codes. You can create a custom Good Guy message tailored to the suggestions in Chapter 10. When you are on the road, you can retrieve messages from a Touch-Tone® phone. You will hear the time and date of the call (1-800-473-5509).

Keeping Business Friends

- Contact-manager software, like Maximizer® from Modatech, stores details about your contacts, a history of meetings, things they like, things you can do for them, and so forth (1-800-804-6299).

- If you have promised to return a call to a friend or a complainer—don't disappoint the individual. I'll Get It! will also answer, screen your calls and give an audio reminder that tells you to call at different intervals during the workday.

- Predictive dialers allow you to save endless time making calls to answering machines or waiting for the phone to be picked up. They can work for an automated Good Guy who needs to make dozens of calls and wants to avoid downtime waiting for busy signals or machines.

- Adopt an ADRMP (auto-dial recorded message player), which can turn from naughty to nice. These are the original pesky little machines that can call lists of numbers and try to sell by computer. They were used in the past as an annoying telemarketing device, but are now much regulated by legislation. Put to better use the ADRMP allows you to deliver hundreds of recorded Good Guy messages automatically, from "happy secretaries' day" to the secretary of a colleague, to "come to our free seminar."

- Callers need not wait on hold. Callback gives callers the option to punch in their number and opt out of holding.

All of the above features and many more can be provided by your phone company. Often they are best identified by calling the small-business service department, which will do a full office analysis. Shop around for hardware.

Handling Bad Guys the Good Guy Way

- If you are online and need some letters, try file name legal.zip. You will get 100 legal form letters, free, that you can tailor to the Good Guy style. In this way, you can add some formality to Milt's admonition in Chapter 13 to keep a lawyer out of a dispute whenever possible. This free set of text files, assembled by Joe Simon, is formatted in ASCII and can be dropped into your word processor.

- A line of inexpensive software called the Perfect series might also fit many of your Good Guy office needs. For example, Perfect Invoice helps you write clear but gentle bill forms that get the job done. The entire series is IBM compatible and is sold from $9.99 to $29.99 in most Office-Max, Office Depot and Staples throughout the country.

Telemarketing Guidelines

The Direct Marketing Association (1-800-243-9069), a must-join group if you are in sales, understands the ethical and legal limits of telemarketing. The association has created guidelines, all in sync with the Good Guy philosophy, for using the superautomated devices set forth above as well as others you'll encounter in your search. A word to the wise . . .

- Telemarketers should promptly disclose to the potential customer their name, the name of their company, and the reason they are calling.

- All telephone offers should be clear, honest and complete. Before offering a certain product at a certain price, the telemarketer should be prepared to substantiate all claims and offers. No offers or solicitations should be made under the pretense of conducting research when the actual intent is to sell products or raise money.

- Telemarketers must disclose the cost of goods and services and all terms and conditions, including payment plans, refund policies, and extra charges such as insurance and shipping and handling, before the customer agrees to buy a product.

- When using automatic dialing equipment, telemarketers should use only equipment that allows the telephone to release the line immediately when the customer disconnects.

- The use of ADRMPs (auto-dial recorded message players) must conform to tariffs and state and local laws. When a telemarketer places a solicitation call, the telemarketer must obtain permission from the customer before the recorded message can be delivered.

- Telemarketers should not tape conversations without first getting the other person's consent.

- Telemarketers should remove from their list the names of anyone who asks, as well as consult the DMA Telephone

Preference Service name removal list. Names on these suppression lists should not be rented or sold.

- Telemarketers should be especially sensitive when speaking with minors and not attempt to sell children products and services designed for adults.

- Telemarketing managers should monitor telemarketing and customer relations conversations only after employees have been informed.

- Telemarketers should not call anyone with an unlisted or unpublished number unless the customer gave that number to the telemarketer.

- Telemarketers should not use random dialing techniques in sales and marketing solicitations.

- Telemarketers should ship merchandise as soon as practical and honor cancellation requests within three days of closing the sale.

- Telemarketers who collect customer data and intend to rent, sell, or exchange this data for direct marketing purposes should inform the customer. Customer requests not to do so should be honored.

- Telemarketers should operate in accordance with the laws and regulations of the U.S. Postal Service, the Federal Communications Commission, the Federal Trade Commission, the Federal Reserve Board, and other applicable laws.

CHAPTER 12

◇

Enhancing the Promotion Opportunities of Your Business

By now, you may be wondering how some of the fundamental tools of getting business—advertising, promotion, public relations, etc.—fit into the Good Guy system. Well, they all do, but with an attitude change. Many types of self-promotion boil down to shouting the loudest, screaming the longest or pestering the most. The Good Guy method requires you to reexamine all that you do now to "get business" and revamp it so that business is "attracted" to you.

Oddly enough, for the genuine Good Guy, this reorientation means working much less hard! If it feels distasteful, don't do it. That's the rule. If it feels pushy and embarrassing, don't do it. On the other hand, if it feels good, helpful, warm and giving, do it.

The system boils down to shining that spotlight on the other guy. That's the Good Guys' fundamental method of self-promotion. Once people get wind of your ability to help them, they will come. That's it, except that you must let this permeate every aspect of your business.

Good Guys Make Spectacular Use of Promotional Opportunities Because They Are Never Opportunists

The world is pretty tired of in-your-face promoters. Whether by mail or in person, the old screaming, pushing and shouting ways are going by the board. People want help, and that's the secret of the Good Guy method. We share a different definition of "opportunity."

In an opportunity, you have a chance to help others. In a business opportunity, you have a chance to help others in business. That's the essence of Good Guy promotion.

Let's say that you are at a party and suddenly are introduced to a "big-wig." Attempting to demonstrate how great you are is a terrible mistake, obnoxious and self-defeating. But so is shyly saying "hello" and disappearing into the herb dip.

If you have the chance to speak about a matter of interest to the newly introduced person, do so. And follow up with no-strings-attached help. If you must force the conversation, don't. It was never an opportunity in the first place.

SILENT SURVEY #12

Please answer these questions:

1. How do I promote my business today?
2. How much do I spend on promotion?
3. What promotion has been the most successful?
4. What has been the least successful?
5. How can I enhance the successful method with a Good Guy approach?

TO DO

Quickly write down a three-line, Good Guy ad for your company—even if you don't advertise in print and never will.

What benefit is your work to the world? That's your lead into self-promotion in any form. Keep that message consistent and don't let anyone influence or direct you down a different path.

Adriane's Newsletter

I know this is not easy. I love my newsletter *Wealthbuilder* as much as you love your company or business. I have about 50 pages of great things I want to say. But what is the true benefit of the letter? What does it do for the reader? Here's my three-line response. It doesn't even provide a name (who cares but me anyway what I call it?).

> "You can make money like a pro, even if you don't know the first thing about investing. All you have to do is read 12 pages a month, 11½, if you don't count the mailing label."

When I look at the words, I notice a fundamental truth. It's not for the already sophisticated and it's not for people who care too little to read a few pages a month. So, I won't promote to them.

What do your three lines reveal to you?

––––––––––––– ◇ –––––––––––––

GOOD GUYISM APPLIED: ADRIANE'S LESSONS IN DIRECT MARKETING

To demonstrate further the idea of spotlighting the needs of others and the benefits of what you do, let's explore what must be the most hyped-up, written-about and difficult-to-grasp area of self-promotion, the sales letter.

The letters discussed in Chapter 6 are written after you have met or spoken with someone. You have some idea of what they want, what you can offer them and, as a Good Guy, you plan to do just that.

But, if you are in sales, and *everyone* is in sales in one way or another, you may be writing to people you've never seen, who have never seen you, and are certainly not expecting your letter.

As a newsletter publisher, I had to learn fast how to write letters that sell. As usual, I hit the books, and also as usual, I was amazed to see that all the best ideas are distilled from the "mother" concept—do something for the other guy. Millions of dollars of direct mail tests, an entire library section at the Direct Marketing Association, all come to the same conclusion.

- Put yourself in the recipient's position.
- Offer what they want, not what you would want.
- State the benefits to them immediately.
- Continue enhancing the benefits throughout the letter.
- Mail the letter in a way that shows respect for them and for what you have to say.

It is that easy. Yet, sales letters are done wrong far too often. Even the veterans whose letters I read for inspiration surprise me by the mistakes they make. When I ask them about it, they always say they were testing other ways of approaching their prospects. In every case, when they do not stick to a form of the Good Guy approach, the test failed.

Here are the Good Guy solutions to every one of the biggest mistakes made in direct marketing letters:

- Don't turn your precious letter into junk mail with white stick-on labels.

    Buy good quality paper and envelopes, and hire a fulfillment house to print the addresses. If you don't have the money, sit down with your mother, husband, wife, lover or next-door neighbor and hand-address the envelopes. Or hire a student. If you have a big mailing, rent a machine or use a computer mail-merge system.

    Labeled mail does not get opened, and it may not even be delivered! The unfortunate results of several investigations reveal that "junk" mail may be discarded by postal workers. Illegal, yes. But believable. Don't let it happen to you.

- Send your letters first class.

  No postage savings is worth the possibility of nearly 20 percent undelivered mail, or mail that can take up to three weeks to reach its destination. Put first-class mail in your budget, and cut down on something else if you must.

- Never lie.

  If there is nothing truthfully good about your product, why are you selling it? Tell all the good points as well as how hard you are working to minimize the bad points.

- Visualize the reader and provide the benefit he or she wants up front in the letter.

  On my radio talk show I can visualize my caller's age, ethnicity, gender and location just by hearing the voice. That gives me clues as to what the caller wants, so I can deliver. You can do the same without the voice. How? By selecting mailing lists that are targeted to certain people.

By targeting, you'll know if the letter is received by people who are over 55, are Hispanic, have just bought a home, or have just had a baby. Pretending to be them, what would you like to be offered if you were? Offer it in the first paragraph of your letter and take it from there.

Here are three examples I use:

1. Headline to sell *Wealthbuilder* newsletter to baby boomers:

   "If you take 25 minutes a month to read *Adriane G. Berg's Wealthbuilder,* you will become at least 20 percent richer every year—guaranteed—or your subscription price back."

   It took lots of time and testing to arrive at that opening. And, it is not appropriate for every reader;

it's for my baby-boomer list. I identify with that group and I know that for them, even more than money, time is of the essence. Hence, the 25 minute comment. (That's how long it takes to read my monthly letter.)

It's an investment letter with a track record. I have testimonials that clients and listeners make about 20 percent, so I can use the figure.

Most important, I refund the $42 subscription price, even after a whole year. Why? Because I so strongly believe that readers will want continued access to the information that they will never ask for money back. For the few who do, I'm a Good Guy. If I have not met their need, I don't want their money.

2. Headline and copy for the over-65 group:

"Now that you are retired, is your money working as hard for you as you worked for it?

"Every dollar you have now represents a little piece of your past—a ball game you didn't attend with your child, a party you missed because you had to work late. No one handed you your money, but lots of folks want you to hand it back.

"I call my newsletter the *Wealthbuilder,* but, I could just as well call it 'Wealthdefender' . . . ."

As a Good Guy, I need to provide different things to this older audience. They like a well-written letter that's heartwarming and interesting. Also, they have more time to read. My newsletter is the same for several audiences, but the premiums and special reports are different.

3. Headline and copy for the under-25 group:

"You may have seen my book *Your Wealthbuilding Years* in your college bookstore. Now that you've graduated, you can get monthly financial guidance at specially reduced rates. And in the next two years I'll help you make so much money that you'll be able to afford to pay full price."

SILENT SURVEY #13

Take a look at the last several paragraphs; they were written in a deliberate way to serve two purposes. First, I wanted to make my point about writing "for the audience." Second, I wanted to set up this next survey. Ask yourself:

Did I become interested in Adriane's newsletter? If so, what did I respond to? Saving time, saving money, bonuses, education? (These are the valuable tips you too can give to others.) Did I think she was trying to sell the letter to me subliminally? Did I feel resentment? Did it turn me off? Watch the delicate balance between selling and opportunism.

As you develop your ideal letter, a million questions will arise. Some of the books in the bibliography will certainly be a big help. Luckily, as we have said, the Good Guy philosophy is self-contained. How would you like to be approached? Are you being polite, ethical, truthful, fair, conscientious in the preparation of your letter?

Sales letters cannot make anyone do what they don't want to do. Phoney manipulation will leave you wondering why no one returned your order form. On the other hand, a sales letter can make individuals buy from you instead of the other guy, and open their eyes to a product or service they did not formerly consider. So, write to give those people the best you have:

- Moneyback guarantees
- Premiums
- Discounts
- Good service
- Special bonuses

They work. Offer them.

A special form of promotional opportunity is the expo, show or convention, covered in Chapter 7. You might want to review that chapter before going on. Following are four sample pages from the 12-page monthly subscription newsletter, *Adriane G. Berg's Wealthbuilder.*

Adriane G. Berg's

WEALTHBUILDER

Getting Rich Is Only Half The Fun!   **No.4 • June 1995**

Hello, Hello, Hello!

In this issue of Wealthbuilder I'm beginning to accomplish the four goals that motivated me to write a newsletter in the first place.

#1-I wanted to bring techniques used by the very wealthy to middle class folks like my family and yours. Because I have been an estate lawyer for 25 years I know how wealthy people invest. The lead article on selling short against the box can make anyone a super-sophisticated investor. It also shows you how to shelter your capital gains. Many people have good stocks that they need to cash out for retirement; but, would suffer a huge tax bite. Grasping the rules of selling short can save the day. It is also a money making alternative for speculators and conservative investors alike.

#2-I wanted to form consortiums, groups with similar investing interests, so we have the same market power that the very wealthy have. In this issue I explain real estate tax liens and ask you if you are interested in pursuing a group investment. You will find these requests frequently as time goes on. I want Wealthbuilder subscribers to become a buying force. Already I have been able to get a Swiss bank to accept $35,000 deposits when their minimum was 1 million! I am meeting with them in Vienna on June 5 and will report in the July issue.

#3-I wanted to have a way to answer your questions. I have so little air time that I hardly scratch the surface in meeting your needs. I'm exploring E mail, tele-conferencing and more. Just keep questions coming.

#4-I wanted to find an economical way to deliver tiffany stamp legal services in trust, estates and asset protection. This is happening with our group seminars outlined on page 8.

Most important, you are part of a growing enterprise that started from scratch, as I have in my real life. I DON'T BELIEVE THAT THE ONE BORN WITH THE SILVER SPOON NEED BE SERVED THE BIGGEST PORTION!

THE ART OF SELLING SHORT FOR PROFIT, HEDGING AND TAX SAVINGS

I f you are not familiar with the short sale, it's the way to make major dollars either at the beginning of bear markets (stocks are going down-we are NOT in such a market) or in bull markets when many stocks are high and there are frequent overvalued prices and price pull backs (we are in such a market right now.) The best part of learning how to sell short is that once you master it, you can use it to make money with stocks, bonds, and many other style securities.

For the non-speculator, most of us (except me), selling short saves taxes on highly appreciated stocks that you already own. Combined with estate planning, it can save you 100% of your capital gains tax. Read on to see how it works:

" ...the strategy is to sell the stock while short because you expect the market price to take a dive."

MAKING MONEY WITH A SHORT SALE

A short sale means that you have sold a security before you even own it. To be "long" a stock means you already own it. To be "short", it's not in your portfolio-as in the idiom "I'm short of cash."

The heart of the strategy is to sell the stock while short because you expect the market price to take a dive. Then buy it and deliver when the price dips neatly below your sale price. Pocket the profit.

As far as your buyer is concerned, the short sale closes on the date of the sale as would any stock purchase transaction. The difference is that the investor (you) borrows the stock from the brokerage house. They, in turn, borrow from an institutional seller.

Let's say you decide that Boston Chicken is about to cross the road to the downside. You sell 10,000 shares at $50. To do this you "borrow" $500,000 worth of BC (let's use big numbers, what the heck!) Now there is actual cash of $500,000 in your account. But, you also owe a debt to the brokerage house of the same amount, for the stock you borrowed. You pay interest at say 5.75%

Subsequently, the stock price drops. You buy it and replace the 10,000 shares, pay the interest with the profit and keep the rest. If you made a mistake and the stock goes up, you must buy at a higher price, replace the stock and take a loss. Selling short is a real money maker when you know how to analyze stocks for Failure. Some popular stocks that traders feel are very overvalued right now are Starbucks, Boston Chicken, and Toys R Us. I go along with the first two.

RESTRICTIONS

• The stock must be available for borrowing-your broker will tell you
• You must pay dividends to the owner of the stock from which the broker borrowed the stock for you
• The stock when sold short must trade on an up or zero tick-a price higher than the previous price or the same price as long as the price

Continued on Page 2

ISSUE HIGHLIGHTS

HOW MUCH UNCLE SAM WANTS TO INHERIT FROM YOU AND WAYS TO DISINHERIT HIM

In the next 5 years over 1 trillion dollars in middle class assets will be inherited, much of it by Uncle Sam. This I attribute to the "I'm not rich enough" attitude of the American middle class toward issues of estate and gift tax.

In 1988 two Philadelphia Inquirer reporters, Bartlett and Steele, won the Pulitzer Prize for uncovering 600 private inheritance tax exemptions voted into the 1986 Internal Revenue Code by various congressmen. No one cared or even took note of this first class scandal. One such exemption applied only to persons from Texas who died at age 75 on Oct 28, 1983, residing in Tarrant County and with estates of under 12.5 million. That allowed the family of a Texas millionaire to keep 4 million dollars, instead of paying Uncle Sam. Still, no one cared.

My friends in the insurance industry tell me that many people refuse insurance because they say "let my kids make it on their own, let them take care of their own future." Ok. maybe so, but what about your past. A government taking of what you've earned in your lifetime wipes out the bounty of your past as well as your children's future. It makes sense to avoid this confiscation, especially when, in fact, it is so easy to do.

The Federal estate tax on $1 million dollars is $153,000, on $2 million it is $588,000. This will get much higher if the Federal estate tax exclusion is ever reduced from the present $600,000 to the $200,000 figure that presently shows up in many proposals on Capital Hill. Nor does this count the extra tax of 15% on large pensions or IRAs.

AVOID THE 4 BIGGEST ESTATE PLANNING TRAPS-THEY ARE

1) believing that the proceeds of a life insurance policy is inherited tax free. Insurance is counted in your gross estate if you die owning the policy, able to change beneficiaries, take loans against it or dictate how dividends are applied
2) giving gifts with strings attached, keeping access to the money, having tacit agreements to give it back. Such "conditional gifts" are still your money according to the IRS..
3) giving a general power of appointment without realizing it-that's the right to decide how someone else's money is to be distributed. For example, if your folks name you beneficiary of a trust and you can decide who gets the money after you die, that trust fund is counted in your estate.
4) thinking that a revocable, so-called "living trust," or probate avoiding trust saves taxes. It doesn't!

THE TWO MOST IMPORTANT THINGS TO DO TO SAVE ESTATE TAXES

1. IF YOU ARE MARRIED, put a clause in your will or probate avoiding trust allowing the trustee or executor to allocate up to the maximum Federal Exclusion to the trust and name your spouse the beneficiary of income and your kids the beneficiary of the principal when your spouse dies. If you can't follow this -don't worry-ask for a credit shelter trust. If your lawyer doesn't know what that is, get another lawyer.
2. IF YOU ARE SINGLE, set up a charitable remainder trust, you will get a big income tax deduction, increase your income stream and get tax free money to your heirs by buying a replacement insurance policy in the amount of the charitable gift. If you cannot buy an economical policy, create a family foundation.

VERY FANCY STUFF

• If you are the founder of a family business sell your common stock over time to the kids in return for a private annuity. IRS tables set up the amount of the annuity depending on age, value of business and more
• Set up an off-shore testamentary trust, the income will escape U.S. taxes if done right
• Sell appreciated assets to kids in installments, it puts a ceiling on amounts kids must pay, whereas private annuity payments continue as long as you live
• Create a grit-give away the property to the kids,

but retain the income-Grantor Retained Annuity Trust -grat
• Hold assets in a family limited partnership as described in the Pocket Lawyer APRIL issue

THE SUCCESS TAX

If you take $150,000 a year from your pension or a lump sum of $750,000 you are subject to a 15% excise tax on any amount over that. Your estate is subject to a 15% tax on any pension accumulation that could yield over $150,000 a year for your actuarial life.
Hints-1)start to withdraw, don't accumulate pensions, 2)leave spouse as beneficiary of pension extending time for slow withdrawal to his or her lifetime

ADDING INSULT TO INJURY

The accumulated pension will also have an income tax payable by the heirs.
Hint-estate taxes are deductible as "income in respect of a decedent." If your accountant doesn't know these rules get another accountant. Provide in your will or trust for the provision of a disclaimer so your heirs can do post mortem tax planning.

DON'T FORGET STATE ESTATE TAX

If you own real estate it will be taxed in both the state in which it is located and perhaps in your state of residence, as well. Hint-transfer real estate to a corporation and own shares in the corporation instead of owning the real estate outright.

THE ULTIMATE SOLUTION

DON'T BE AFRAID OF INSURANCE. Second to die policies are economical. If you are a two paycheck couple with dependent kids consider a first to die policy. The entire death benefit is paid when the first one dies.
Books to read-"WARNING:DYING MAY BE HAZARDOUS TO YOUR WEALTH" CAREER PRESS 1-800-955-7272, $16.99, 1995 WRITTEN BY ME.
IRS FORM 706-free from METLIFE, a good book on how to fill out the estate tax return, ask for METLIFE T 10540(07-91) METLIFE, One Madison Avenue, New York, New York 10010-3690; order the estate planning tapes "SAVING THE FAMILY FORTUNE" offered at a discount to WEALTHBUILDER subscribers on page 5.

ISSN # 1081-1532 TITLE:ADRIANE G. BERG'S "WEALTHBUILDER"© 1995, MONTHLY PUBLICATION, PUBLISHED BY BOCHNER FAMILY LIMITED PARTNERSHIP, 143 U.S. Route 206 South,Chester, New Jersey 07930. CIR. 4000

Herewith rapid fire Q&A to keep up with your questions. Please don't call with questions-can't answer by phone.
Just write to address on back page. Thanks..

WHAT'S DOING WITH SILVER?
For Mort-
Don't sell your junk coins in the cans, it's time to keep them. I expect price of silver to hit over $6.00 an ounce.

DOW DIVIDEND STRATEGY
For Andrew-
The mutual fund that follows the Dow Dividend Strategy is Select 10, see page 6. Merrill not Dreyfus has the fund or call Libman, number on page 6.

HOW TO USE THE PORTFOLIO ON PAGE 6-7
For Walter-
The model Wealthbuilder Portfolio has 25% invested in high quality bonds. Walter wants to know if this is in addition to the amount of bonds he purchases to maintain his income.
    The answer is no. If you already have high quality bonds to sustain your lifestyle count them toward the 25 %. If they come out to more than the 25% and you still need them to give you the income stream that pays the rent, adjust the equity portion of the model portfolio down.

403B
For Linda-
Do NOT roll over your 403b into a private mutual fund IRA. The 403b has borrowing and other advantages that you will ruin with an improper roll over. The rates given by phone are the accurate rates. As for your allocation of 50/50-only a financial planner can help you. The king of the 403b is Michael Mathias he is reachable at 1-914-99722900. Call and say I sent you. I receive no compensation if you call him and I'LL NEVER REALLY KNOW IF YOU CALLED. (Michael keeps his files confidential—so, as Jackie Mason would say, "it's up to you."

BEARER BOND RULES

For Tessie-
Bearer bonds were to have been traded in for registered bonds on 1991. Too many folks were cashing them in anonymously for the comfort of the IRS. IF YOU STILL HAVE BEARER BONDS NO ONE WILL INFORM YOU IF THEY ARE CALLED, YOU MAY LOSE INTEREST. Unless you plan to evade taxes, speak to a bond broker about whether they should be registered.

HOW LONG IS LONG TERM?
For Marie-
As for short or long term lending-I would like you to type out your question and resend it to the address on the back. I am thinking of making it am entire article in August. For now, any time you buy a bond from a municipality, corporation, or the U.S. treasury or when you buy a C.D. from a bank or brokerage house consider 1-3 years=short term lending; 3-8 years=intermediate term; 8 years plus=long term.

WILL WE HAVE A FLAT TAX? SHOULD I SELL MY MUNIS?
For George-
Who asks whether a flat tax would diminish the value of municipal bonds and tax deferred investments like annuities. This is purely a political question since no flat tax is in existence, yet. My feeling is that municipalities and the insurance industry have two of the most significant lobbies in the U.S. Do NOT go out of munis in anticipation of a flat tax if they are otherwise right for you. I'm still investigating.

HEY! DON'T FORGET!!!

Don't forget 5% of your WEALTHBUILDER portfolio belongs in metals. I am very light on tangibles, but; I believe that many people have mistakenly abandoned them. Asia, especially India, is demanding silver and gold for artifacts, jewelry and manufacturing. Either buy coins try my friend Michael Checkan of INTERNATIONAL FINANCIAL CONSULTANTS see column left OR JUST HOARD JUNK SILVER FROM FLEA MARKETS (ODD COINS, SPOONS, PLATES) ETC. You won't go wrong.

WHERE IS ADRIANE?

JUNE SEMINARS

6/6-WHITE PLAINS , NEW YORK
INTERSTATE FINANCIAL-INVESTING AND ESTATE PLANNING

6/14-HOFSTRA UNIVERSITY, LONG ISLAND
ARS AND FRIEDLAND, FISHBEIN, LAIFER & ROBBINS
ASSET PROTECTION-DOMESTIC AND OFF-SHORE

SPECIAL INTEREST

▲ If you have any chance of getting college aid keep your kid's college money in your name not theirs. But, if college aid is impossible, keep it in their name to save taxes. How do you know if you have a shot at aid? Rule: THE TWO STAFFORD LOAN PROGRAMS ALLOW AID FOR FAMILIES WITH $70,000 INCOME, MORE IF YOU HAVE SEVERAL KIDS OF COLLEGE AGE. Get me a cold compress.

▲ 1995 Social Security cost of living index rose 2.8% (minimal). So, how much do our seniors get? Average couple $1,178, single $656 a month. I just came back from Jamaica which has $3.00 a week social security for seniors. Their living conditions? DON'T ASK. Just go out and kiss our flag.

▲ Many of you have asked whether you can invest in foreign currency with traveler's checks. A good idea. Am Ex checks are available in British pounds, Canadian dollars, French francs, Japanese yen and German marks. Now you can diversify outside the dollar a few hundred dollars at a time. These are not nearly as good as the money markets and currency accounts that give interest. But, they are swell if you plan to travel abroad soon and, as I believe, will face an even weaker dollar or you just have $500 to invest and can't meet the minimums of currency accounts. Go to your bank or call Michael Checkan (I know plugging him gets annoying but the field of currency is treacherous so when I meet an honest guy I get excited) 1-800-831-0007 besides he has a Swiss traveler's check program for small investors.

HOW TO MAIL IN YOUR QUESTIONS

~

The lifeblood of ADRIANE G. BERG'S "WEALTHBUILDER" ARE YOUR QUESTIONS. DON'T HESITATE TO WRITE. Use your own stationary and fill in the following information:

1. State the question first, with no facts given.

2. Provide a succinct set of facts and state dates when events occurred.

3. If professionals have already answered your question , state their answer.

4. State whether you give permission to forward your question to the professional of Adriane's choice, as long as it is cost free to you. BELIEVE IT OR NOT ADRIANE DOESN'T ALWAYS HAVE ALL THE ANSWERS.

5. State if you want a referral to a paid professional for ongoing help.

6. Enclose copies only (no originals) of relevant documents. Do not send court pleadings or lengthy documents. If the information is important paraphrase in your letter.

BE AWARE THAT YOUR QUESTION MAY BE ANSWERED IN THE NEWSLETTER ITSELF, BUT YOUR REAL NAME WILL NEVER APPEAR.

IN NEXT MONTHS ISSUE:

✔ **PENSION PROTECTION ABROAD**

✔ **HOW TO GET 10% YIELD-PLAIN AND SIMPLE**

✔ **TWO GREAT SMALL CAP STOCKS**

✔ **FOREIGN BONDS FOR INCOME INVESTORS**

✔ **HOW EQUITY SWAPS WORK**

✔ **FAKING IT RICH IN THE OFFICE**

✔ **AND MUCH MORE!**

Adriane G. Berg's

WEALTHBUILDER

143 U.S. ROUTE 206 SOUTH
CHESTER, N.J. 07930

FIRST CLASS
POSTAGE & FEES
PAID
DIRECT RESPONSE
MARKETING, INC.

Getting Rich Is Only Half The Fun!

CHAPTER 13

◇

Dealing with Bad Guys and Avoiding the Pitfalls

Warning: How To Spot the Bad Guys and Escape Traps, Backslides and Contamination

While the Good Guys of the world patiently follow the ethical, giving, high-road path to success and wealth, they are outnumbered by Bad Guys seeking a faster buck and willing to sacrifice ethics, truth, and reputation for the day's harvest! In the business world, we often feel surrounded by individuals and firms who bend the truth, issue phony claims and promises, and break only Ten Commandments because there are not Twenty Commandments.

What's the best way to recognize and cope with the Bad Guys, who think their behavior is the norm and that "everybody does it!"?

The single most important rule is this very old adage:

"Fool me once . . . shame on you! Fool me twice . . . shame on me!"

The following story is true, though hard to believe.

A few years ago, a personal friend who is a highly successful professional called Milt with this story:

"Milt, I'm calling because I know you publish a jewelry magazine, and you must be familiar with the diamond business.

133

"Three weeks ago, I got a call about great opportunities in diamond investment. They told me that diamond prices have been going up for years, and are controlled by a national cartel (DeBeers). They said diamonds are better than gold, easy to lock up, and a great hedge against inflation.

"I bought a first $25,000 in investment-grade diamonds, and they were delivered last Monday. But I got suspicious because they were encased in plastic, with a warning not to open for three years, or the money-back guarantee would be invalidated. Milt, what do you think?"

This was Milt's reply:

- "This is a typical boiler room (high-pressure salesmen in a telephone bank, calling a sucker list of wealthy but potentially naive clients).

- "All diamonds are not alike. They have so many variations that each must be appraised individually.

- "The 'do not open' clause prevents fair appraisal.

- "Whether now or three years later, you probably will discover that the diamonds have no value near what you paid; and I doubt you can get your money back."

The victim was so disappointed that he called the "boiler room" to demand an explanation. A few days later, he confessed to Milt that they had "taken" him for a second investment of another $15,000!

This is not unique. Many Bad Guys do well for a while. They're not always easy to recognize; they have perfected their methods; and our response is not always as informed or immediate as it should be. So this chapter will contain guidelines that you may find applicable to Bad Guys, whether employers, employees, suppliers, customers or anyone else in the business world who displays the following characteristics or "Smoke Signals."

The individual:

1. is unwilling to confirm in writing what was stated verbally;

2. breaks any promise, however trivial, and then denies the promise was made;

3. first contacted disappears, or is unavailable, and is replaced by another person who claims ignorance of what the first person promised or told you;

4. pressures you to make an immediate decision, lest the alleged opportunity disappear forever;

5. solicits you to participate in an unethical or illegal transaction, which would be costly to a third party (phantom bill; kickback; padded insurance claims, etc.);

6. asks you to send a check to an individual name in payment for a transaction with a business firm;

7. quotes a price so ridiculously low that it is "too good to be true";

8. adopts a business firm identification that is a look-alike or sound-alike with the name of a better established and more reputable firm in the same business;

9. seeks your business but makes disparaging remarks about his former employer or current competitors in the same field;

10. uses a box number and you cannot find a business address;

11. promises to correct an error or defect, but misses the agreed upon deadline;

12. can be reached only through a 900 number, so that the contact is making money on your conversation.

Although each "smoke signal" listed above may require different handling, here are some rules applicable to many such situations.

• Show the "contact" that you are writing down notes on a verbal discussion.

- Confirm immediately in writing the details and conclusions of any such conversation.

- Don't be embarrassed to ask questions indicating that you are cautious or suspicious.

- When necessary, send a certified letter summarizing what has been agreed upon, with a deadline for action or the information you expect in reply.

- Discontinue new business with the individual or firm until satisfied.

- Never prematurely send money, give your credit card number, or verbally confirm any transaction unless your suspicions and requests for further information have been satisfied.

- Don't be maneuvered as an employee into inappropriate behavior (even under employer pressure) with the explanation that ". . . everybody does it." Good Guys don't!

- Get to the real person in charge quickly, if the behavior of the intermediary is suspicious or unsatisfactory.

- Never give your trust a second time to the individual who has fooled you once! Look for Good Guy behavior that matches your own standards.

What If You Really Want To Be a Good Guy and Your Employer Turns Out To Be a Bad Guy?

Sooner or later, some Good Guys find they're working for Bad Guys. Here's a true example, and some sound advice on how to handle it.

A widow, Betty R., slowly returned to the business world as her children matured. She became associated part-time with a travel agency. She gradually built a personal clientele and increased her income, gaining experience while catering carefully to the needs, interests and budgets of her clients.

With growing referrals and a developing following, Betty sensed a promising career. Eventually she joined the agency full-time.

She soon discovered a questionable practice of which she was previously unaware. The agency advertised a super-bargain vacation package deal. She and the other agents were instructed to handle all inquiries by getting a credit card number, imposing a fee, and telling the caller that an effort would be made to book the trip. Later, the agent would call the prospect, state that the trip was "sold out" (it was never available) and try to switch to a higher-priced available package.

Betty was also instructed that if clients protested and attempted to cancel, the agency would be unable to reverse the initial service charge on their credit cards, and might be unable to provide adequate travel accommodations on shorter notice. So, some clients would eventually buy the second package.

When Betty told her boss she had never done anything like this before, she was told "Everybody does it; this is standard practice in the highly competitive travel business."

Betty now faced a dilemma: An instinctive Good Guy, invited to go along with the behavior of an unethical Bad Guy employer, begins wondering about the alternative. Here's Milt's answer:

"First, decide whether you want to be a Good Guy or Bad Guy for the rest of your business life. Once you rationalize and begin improper behavior, you'll find it almost impossible to turn back.

"Ask your Bad Guy employer to put in writing the shady instructions that have been given to you verbally. Of course, he will refuse.

"Start a private, confidential folder giving dates and details of the improper behavior that you were invited or required to follow. This is your helpful defense in the event of a subsequent unjust dismissal or difficulty.

"Start looking for similar employment with a Good Guy in the same business or in a related field where your experience would be useful. Maybe your experience, and your instinctive reluctance to behave unethically, will become desirable assets to the right firm.

"Meanwhile, when pressured to condone or participate in improper behavior, politely decline. If you can afford to leave immediately, do so. If you cannot, hang on until you find something better. But meanwhile, do not get involved, even temporarily, in Bad Guy behavior.

"You have only one business life to lead. Because you have picked up this book and read this far, we hope you're convinced you cannot lead the Good Guy life in a Bad Guy's business. Make up your mind immediately that nothing will change unless you change it!"

Losers and Leeches— A Special Kind of Bad Guy

Not every kind of Bad Guy who can seriously damage you is overtly out to get you. Especially if you appear to be a winner, there will be those who admire, even adore you, and therefore "want a piece of you." In the extreme, celebrities experience these Bad Guys as stalkers, overzealous fans and others who insinuate themselves in their life and can ruin them.

Some such Bad Guys are clear losers who constantly ask for handouts and prey upon your good nature. Handling them is simple. Give money, but *don't give them jobs*. Sad sacks are not for you. Although many a Good Guy also has a bit of the teacher, preacher or reformer, probably you can't help as an employer.

Follow this rule: If someone who is an obvious loser wants a position in your business that can affect the business, *just say no*. If the need is financial help, it's up to you. Most likely you are inviting a lifetime of dependency, but guilt may get you.

Even Abraham Lincoln eventually had to turn down his brother for a handout. In the Library of Congress is the historic letter he wrote, containing the message: "I'll give you one dollar for every dollar you earn, but nothing if you earn nothing."

If you are the perpetual soft touch, and many Good Guys are, you may find that, after reading Chapter 15 and starting some organized charitable work, it is easier to refuse the losers and leeches of this world. After all, you will have a well-thought-out outlet for your charitable spirit.

Another Bad Guy type wears an even tougher disguise. That is the person who offers you a partnership, a joint venture or another side-by-side work arrangement, when his or her energy, capital, contacts, clout are far inferior to yours. If you accept, it is usually because this Bad Guy presses one of your "hot buttons." Are you overworked, ignoring an aspect of your own or a related business, hoping to find a clone, or finding that you dislike managing? What's in it for you after all is said and done? If you know yourself—your needs and shortcomings—well enough, individuals cannot aggrandize themselves just by filling a small need.

Many times, equal partnerships are formed between real successes and real losers because the loser was smart enough to press the hot button. In all cases, you will not fall prey to any kind of Bad Guy if you understand your possible vulnerability.

SILENT SURVEY #14

Please respond with "yes," "no" or an answer to the following:

- I'm a little greedy. _____
- I'm a little lazy. _____
- I'm a little timid. _____
- I'm not one who likes to hire, fire, manage. _____
- I don't like detail work. _____
- I don't like selling. _____
- I don't like staying in the office. _____
- I don't like constant travel. _____

- Anything else? _____
- I am vulnerable to giving away too much to someone who unburdens me from _____ or offers me _____.
- A better way to help myself is _____ (hire someone, take a training course, etc.).

---◇---

GOOD GUYISM APPLIED:
ADRIANE EXPLAINS HOW
TO AVOID TEMPTATION AND MAKE
A FORTUNE AT THE SAME TIME

My field of financial journalism can be a hotbed of temptation for anyone. A single word for or against an insurance product, a stock, a real estate investment can be make—or break—it for interested parties. I have been offered just about everything to "put in a good word," write a favorable article, push a fringy product.

I never have, and it's my most important claim to fame. In *Othello,* Shakespeare referred to "Good name in man and woman . . ." That's what's valuable. And as I watch others in my field fade from the scene, I 'm painfully aware of how easy it is to succumb to the promise of a fast buck.

How do I stay "clean"? Simple: I weigh the "haunt factor." The haunt factor is probably the best measure of whether or not to participate in any moneymaking venture. Will it haunt you someday? If so why? When? How often? And how much?

This is not ethics: I leave that for the philosphers and clergy. This is self-preservation. I want to keep that still center of peacefulness to value and enjoy every once in a while, and I can't if I'm haunted.

In my case, haunting comes easily. Of course, there are probably a few good, honest deals I could have made or recommended to others that were quashed by the "haunt test." So be it. What I gained was better—a good night's sleep. And, that's not all: I gained a career that won't blow away.

As other people lose sponsors, I gain them. As others lose face, I strengthen my acceptance. An agent once said to me in amazement, "No one has a bad word for you. How do you do it?" That's just it—I do less, take less, act slower and with more caution. It comes down to cultivating Milt's original rule of patience.

SILENT SURVEY #15

Please answer these questions:

1. Is there an aspect of my business in which I am vulnerable to corruption?
2. What happens if I don't give in?
3. What happens if I do?
4. Have I capitulated, even in a minor way, with Bad Guys? When? Why? Was it worth it? What happens if I stop?
5. How can I extricate myself from the Bad Guys now? What price will I pay?

TO DO

If you have a serious need to disembroil yourself from a bad situation, make a plan. Follow the plan.

How To Escape Undamaged When Bad Guys Threaten Lawsuits (a Word from Milt)

We live in a "litigious society." Lawsuits are a way of life. No day passes without thousands of angry phone calls or "lawyer letters" in which Party A threatens to sue Party B for real, exaggerated or completely imaginary damages.

Once you get sued, it's going to cost you . . . lost time, endless court actions, legal fees, and depositions, witnesses and papers. No matter who wins, everybody ultimately loses . . . except the lawyers!

So your real goal, when you get a lawyer's call or a threat, is to AVOID GETTING SUED.

My first such lawsuit, completely without merit on the part of the plaintiff (the Bad Guy who sued our company), cost us as innocent defendants over $20,000 in legal fees during four years of moves and countermoves. The plaintiff ultimately settled for $1 (yes . . . one dollar!).

We then started a defense mechanism that applied forever. And we never had another costly lawsuit. Here it is:

1. Get the word out to every employee that, as soon as anyone says a threatening word ("damage" . . . "sue" . . . "lawyer"), it must be referred to top management. Don't let an argumentative employee trigger a lawsuit before the dispute reaches you.

2. If you receive a threatening "lawyer letter," don't call your lawyer just because the other guy demands it. Lawyers take over and send you to the sidelines. Too often they heat up the dispute by quickly becoming argumentative.

3. Reply quickly, and don't argue. Apologize for any unintended offenses. Do not admit total guilt. Offer reasonable solutions and adjustments. Give the other guy a reasonable "out." (See Chapter 9 on handling complaints.)

4. Give the lawyer and/or the client attention "from the top" of your firm.

5. If the offered resolution doesn't satisfy your adversary, continue negotiating. You may consult a lawyer for advice, but keep him or her out of the direct negotiations unless you are actually sued.

6. On the rare occasions that this strategy fails, and your adversary still sounds serious about suing, use the following final response:

```
Dear Mr. xxxxxxxxxxxxxxx:
    We hope you'll reconsider your intended
lawsuit. It would be terribly costly and
time-consuming to all parties.
    A lawsuit would force us to defend
vigorously. Once we retain a lawyer, we
would countersue. We believe your case is
without merit, so we would demand, from
you and your lawyer, reimbursement of all
our costs on the basis of frivolous
litigation. Why subject yourselves to this
added cost in a dubious lawsuit?
```

(I'm confident that this added defensive strategy has caused dozens of plaintiffs and their lawyers to have a change of heart! It's certainly worked for us.)

Avoiding Lawsuits in a Treacherous World (a Word from Adriane)

As a lawyer for 25 years, I can't be as sanguine as Milt about forestalling lawsuits. Some Bad Guys make suing others their business, and some won't go away no matter what. I will say that the Good Guy approach will not only serve to diminish the number of suits, but will also make you a better litigant if you are sued. In that situation, some of the hidden benefits of the Good Guy system come through for you:

- Everything is in writing. You have a good record, admissible as a contemporaneous writing.

- Your memory can be refreshed and make you strong on the facts because of your record keeping.

- Your case against the Bad Guy is called a "counterclaim" and often results in the mutual withdrawal of claims.

- Your witnesses will like you, want to help you, and be forthcoming; nothing is worse than a reluctant witness.

- Most of all, you will be so nurtured by your Good Guy experiences that you will be able emotionally to withstand the stress of legal battle.

CHAPTER 14

◇

How To Succeed in Your New Job Search by Trying Harder and Working Smarter

Every year finds millions of Americans looking for a first job or a new job, and dreaming of better income and a positive career.

This includes new graduates, other youths reaching maturity, mid-life women entering the job market, adults suddenly unemployed because of corporate or industry changes, and others just seeking a positive career change.

Unfortunately, many are discouraged too easily by reports of job shortages and intense competition in the employment marketplace.

Here's the truth. Attrition, job changes and other factors cause an annual turnover as high as 20 percent in business and industry. That means millions of job opening opportunities each year. With energy and the right strategy, you can make one of them yours.

This chapter recommends effective strategy in four critical areas: your personal resume; the search for an opening; the job interview; and the interview follow-up.

1. Resume Contents . . . and Two Are Better Than One!

Your personal resume is usually the prospective employer's first "look" at you. I recommend two slightly varied approaches:

One resume should be general, summarizing the usual data on name, address, work and educational experience, strengths, etc.

The second should be attuned to a field in which you have a special ambition and qualifications. This resume should contain a statement preferring a career in that field, with background on your strengths related to that career.

The first resume goes to employment agencies, blind ads, employers in varied fields, and is used in the general "networking" process. The specialized resume goes to employers and anyone with connections to the field of your special career interest.

Although I (Milt) know many who have successfully used this unique two-resume strategy, my favorite example is the experience of my youngest son Dennis, a 1982 college graduate with a general education. The very first specialized (real estate sales) resume he mailed found an open door and he began a career he's pursued successfully for 13 years!

Other resume tips:

- *Include a "personal statement" along with the routine information.* State that you want to work hard; you want to continue learning; and you want to join a highly successful company. Employers are looking for recruits with those attitudes.

- *Include clues to your age and marital status.* Employers are not legally permitted to ask those questions, but they are still curious! There's no law against your offering this information, and your candor may make a difference.

- *Mention availability . . . special qualities . . . anything a prospective employer would want to know.*

- *Tell the truth*. False or exaggerated resume claims are suicide for Good Guy careers. Either you'll be discovered, or you'll develop a habit of being a liar!

2. Finding the Right Open Door

The more doors you open or attempt to open, the more likely you'll get an interview with the company offering the right career. Don't confine your search to one strategy; use them all:

- *Answer ads* . . . but even if it's a "blind ad" (advertiser unidentified), send a "cover letter" with your resume. Relate your qualifications and skills to the ad's job description.

- *Approach employment agencies*. Send copies of both resumes, and ask for a personal interview with the placement person(s). Don't sign up with an agency that won't give you a serious interview.

- *Network* through multiple sources. Approach (verbally and with resume copies) school placement offices, business-oriented friends and relatives, business clubs, any contact you might have. But use these only to find an open door, never as excessive "influence"—which causes resentment!

- *Do not waste large fees* on commercial "job strategy services" that make exaggerated promises and require an up-front payment. This field is relatively unregulated, and exploitation of the unemployed has been frequent.

- *Approach desirable employers even when they are not hiring*. Successful firms with a positive environment and first-rate training programs rarely have to advertise. They have files of applicants waiting to be contacted. Call and write, send resumes, find out who interviews, and be politely persistent. Identify these "A" employers and keep after them.

- *Start early!* The college grad or job-market returnee who starts searching very late will find he or she is at the end of a very long line. A new job is a life milestone! Give it the preparation and planning that the search requires!

3. Interview Strategy as Your Career Hangs in the Balance

Although resume contents help to open doors, it's the personal interview where your fate and Good Guy career future are decided. Here's the recommended strategy:

- *Don't dress to extremes.* While "sloppy" is suicidal, it's almost as bad to look like you're 10 minutes out of the clothing store. It's a message with the wrong emphasis.

- *Pre-scout the target.* Who is this company? What are its products and strengths? What's its history and background? Find out in advance from community sources, an anonymous "scouting trip" to the plant or office, company literature, business or banking sources, or someone else "in the know." Be prepared to drop this information during the interview. Someone may ask you why you want to work for this firm. An informed response will be more effective than: "Uh . . . I need a job."

- *Get the interviewer's name right.* Early in the interview, repeat his or her name and ask if the pronunciation and spelling are right. Mispronunciation or misspelling will not score points!

- *Take notes.* It helps in the follow-up letter, and it's usually impressive to the interviewer.

- *Answer questions with brief added information.* Your interviewer wants to hear you talking. Five-word answers to every question won't help.

- *Ask questions of your own.* Ask for a more complete job description, the identity of this job's supervisor, and about training and learning opportunities.

- *Politely ask who else is involved in hiring.* In a small firm, you may be speaking directly to the owner or partner who is the decider. In a larger firm, a personnel manager screens multiple candidates, and presents two or three leading applicants to the decider, who makes the final choice. The diplomatic question to ask your interviewer: Mr. xxxxxxx, is there anyone else involved in the final hiring decision?" The answer gives you the decider's name for further strategy and a copy of your follow-up letter.

- *Politely ask for the job.* When the interviewer's questions are over, compare your qualifications to the job description, show enthusiasm for learning the rest quickly, and state that you're eager to start. You'll score points, even though the screener usually will reply: "We're still interviewing."

- *Politely offer to see the decider.* Example: "Ms. xxxxxxx, before I leave, I wonder if I could have a moment to meet the supervisor of this job, just to say 'hello'." If you're turned down, you haven't lost anything. If you succeed, that's strong evidence you're a finalist for the job.

4. The Follow-Up Letter: How To Outshine Other Job Candidates

The follow-up letter is a super opportunity to gain a big edge on other candidates for the job you want.

Many job applicants send no follow-up letter at all after a job interview, while others send a letter without thinking of the strong impression made by *immediacy.*

You can score points at a critical moment with a strong follow-up letter mailed *within 24 hours*—to both the screener and the decider. Here's the best structure of that letter:

- *What you saw and liked about the company.* Refer to the general atmosphere, the people, the positive signs, training programs, etc.

- *Repeat the primary job description and why you qualify.* Look over your interview notes, summarize what you can handle, and repeat your zest for learning the rest.

- *Repeat your availability on short notice.* In view of the active interviewing, the employer needs someone soon. You're eager to start!

- *Mention decider's name diplomatically.* Whether you met the decider or not during the interview, the follow-up letter gets more of the decider's attention if his or her name is mentioned.

Take a look at the imaginary sample follow-up letter after the next section. Try mailing something like this *at the post office* within a few hours after the interview. Then imagine the following scenario at the company office, the next day. It could happen!

5. What Could Happen After Your Positive Interview and Follow-Up

The busy decider visits the personnel screener.

Decider: "How are we doing on getting that trainee my department needs?"

Screener: "We're still interviewing."

D: "How about Ms. xxxx, who came in yesterday? Look at this terrific letter she just sent! She sounds ready to go!"

S: "Yes, she's a finalist. But I'm seeing two more good ones soon."

D: "Dammit, my whole department is overworked! Why are we still looking when we have found what we want? How about calling xxxxx and telling her to come in starting Monday?"

S: "Okay if you say so! I was just doing my job."

Try This Structure in Your Interview Follow-Up Letter To Get a Big Edge on Other Applicants for the Job

Dear Mr. xxxxxxxxxxxxx:

During my visit this morning, I was particularly impressed by the morale throughout the office, as well as your own focus on high-performance people.

What impressed you at the employer's firm?

I arrived early, in order to read some of your company's literature and the latest company newsletter. I saw success and growth all over the place!

You're ready for most of the job, and will learn the rest.

I've reviewed my notes on your job description. I suspect I'm over 80 percent qualified, and I can't wait to start learning the rest! You have a workplace where I can work and learn with pride. I'm ready to start when I get your call!

You're available immediately or soon.

I was happy for the brief opportunity to meet XXXXX, my prospective supervisor.

Mention prospective supervisor by name.

Or

I'm sorry I didn't have a chance to meet XXXXX, my prospective supervisor. I hope I will have this opportunity soon.

Sincerely,

XXXXXXXXXXXXXX

CHAPTER 15

◇

Taking the Good Guy Approach in Tough Situations

As this book draws to a close, we recognize that the challenges faced by individuals in a particular industry, company or sticky situation may benefit from additional insights drawn from Milt's extensive business experience. What follows is a series of tough questions posed by Adriane and answered by Milt. If you have additional questions or tough situations you'd like us to consider, write to Milton Gralla or Adriane Berg, c/o Dearborn Trade, 155 N. Wacker Drive, Chicago, IL. 60606-1719.

Q. In your organization, patience and "account cultivation" were encouraged and rewarded. But in other fields, including one (insurance) in which I was once involved, there are strict sales quotas, and performance is judged by results every month. How can the Good Guy be a success in that setting?

A. I don't like organizations whose quotas place excessive immediate stress on the individual to be a sprinter rather than a marathoner. Our own company, and others I have seen as most healthy and successful, gave primary emphasis to long-term business, with constant classes and seminars to improve skills. The sales person who becomes "too busy" meeting the quota has no time for long-term cultivation or

153

learning to do the job better. In every field, including insurance, there are companies who share this vision.

Q. How do you follow up your "Good Guy letter" if it remains unacknowledged?

A. Don't assume there are no results. Most positive letters make a dent in the armor of important decision makers. Remain in touch only when you have still another "goodie" to enrich the business of that target, but don't make the mistake of repeating the same first letter because it was unanswered. You are "playing the averages." Not every target will respond, but certainly some blooms will emerge from the planting of many positive seeds.

Q. Similarly, what if you distribute a newsletter, and the recipient(s) neither take action nor contact you further?

A. Patience! First, diplomatically question some of your clients and prospects, from time to time, on whether they are receiving the newsletter, as well as what they like and don't like about it. Second, be sure to place one or more "free offers" of help or information in each newsletter, so that you can evaluate the response. (See Chapter 8 on newsletters). If you are generating no response at all, reexamine the content and format. Good newsletters, if informative and noncommercial, eventually penetrate to the attention and confidence of otherwise unreachable decision makers.

Q. How do you handle a situation in which your partner is a Bad Guy?

A. Partnerships become bad news more than 90 percent of the time. A partnership requires a very rare combination of diplomacy, sacrifice, tolerance, complimentary talents and other assets. A partnership can have many strengths, but may collapse as a result of a single "fatal flaw," much like a chain with many strong links and just one weak link. If in doubt, don't start a partnership in the first place! If you have a partnership and a weak link appears, it becomes an emotional matter rather than a business matter, and soon whole families and other third parties are involved. Every partnership must have very strong escape clauses and arbitration clauses (as in employing relatives, discussed in Chapter 5).

Q. How does a Good Guy collect debts and accounts receivable? Believe it or not, of all my fields of experience, this problem is felt most by lawyers who often get resistance from clients even when a good job is acknowledged.

A. I was lucky to have my brother Larry handling this end of the business, but I can summarize our joint philosophy. You can't stay in business taking too much nonsense from deadbeats who get first-rate products or services and then decline to pay. Use the usual series of prompt collection letters, and then go to a collection agency or some other tough legal alternative. When people called me about our company's tough collection procedures, I replied that I sympathized, but could not pay my printer, the post office, or our employees with only clients' valid explanations. You can have an easier and more profitable life by notifying the worst-paying 5 or 10 percent of your clients to pay up or evaporate.

Q. All entrepreneurs, particularly if they're growing, find themselves negotiating constantly. What is a Good Guy approach in negotiating, such as an office lease, office equipment contract, etc. Is this the time to get tough for a better deal?

A. No! The best price is not always the lowest price! Whenever you squeeze a supplier too hard, you force him to cut corners. Follow the policy that "the best deal is one that is healthy for both parties on a long-term basis." You want your supplier to make a profit from you and to value you, while you also want to be assured the price is competitive. Never squeeze for the last ounce of blood, because you will pay it back sooner or later!

Q. Good Guys often have trouble asking for things, even if they are well deserved. How does a Good Guy set the stage to get a raise, a bonus, a promotion?

A. First, be sure you get to the right person, the one who is the ultimate decision maker. Avoid confrontation with an intermediary who cannot make a "yes" decision. Second, enter the meeting with confidence, evidence, proof of performance. Finally, ask in advance for an adequate amount of time, lest the other party start watching the clock after a few moments. If you cannot be promised adequate time for the meeting, accept a later appointment when you are guaranteed adequate attention and decision. In any hurried meeting where the other party opts to delay to another date, you have lost an important Round One.

Q. How can we use Good Guy techniques to be hired for a job in a competitive market?

A. See the separate chapter on this topic. But in summary: Be sure your resume includes a "personal statement" stating your willingness to work and learn. Get information on your prospective employer before the interview, so as to be fully informed. During the interview, ask a few questions in addition to answering those posed by the interviewer. Diplomatically try to find out if the interviewer is a "screener" or a "decider," and be sure that your follow-up letter goes to both parties. Within 24 hours after the interview, send an honest follow-up letter, stating what you liked, why you qualify, and your willingness to learn all needed new skills. Remember also that you are just one person looking for one job, and a soft or competitive market will not make a difference if you are persistent.

Q. Bill Gates (Microsoft) is considered a Good Guy, in addition to being the richest man in America. He asserts that his employees took no money for six months to help his business grow. What's your reaction?

A. This is impossible to answer, because all the facts may not have been revealed. Did the employees get stock? Was there a specific agreement that they would be repaid a certain sum at a later date? Were they gainfully employed at other jobs, doing the work for Gates "on the side" in hope of future reward? No-pay "jobs" are illegal and inhumane, since a thousand new enterprises go bust for every one that becomes a Microsoft, and the employees are left in the lurch just as if they had bet their last dollars on the lottery. I recommend other options in order to cultivate the dedication and loyalty of employees, including recognition, support of positive behavior, constant training, development of new challenges, goodies such as profit sharing and stock options, an open door to top executives, etc. See Chapter 3, "Selecting, Enriching and Empowering Your Good Guy Team."

Q. How does a Good Guy handle unfair competition? We find this in everyday life, in politics, and certainly in business. What's the best response to unfair business competition?

A. Forget about complaining to the government, the prosecutors, or the regulatory authorities. They are understaffed, overworked, and unwilling to respond to matters they regard as commercial competition, even if illegal behavior is apparent. Second, don't make a career of responding to the phonies and liars, because you will succeed only in giving them more attention. Good Guy victims of such behavior should puncture and lampoon some of the Bad Guy's more ridiculous and incredible behavior without even mentioning a name. For example, I would place a paragraph or two in a newsletter to all my clients and prospects, heaping ridicule and destroying the credibility of—without naming—the Bad Guy.

In more serious cases where the behavior is persistent and truly damaging, I suggest a "lawyer letter" advising the Bad Guy of the possible damage caused by his illegal behavior, and the intent to sue for not only actual damages but also punitive damages. Save up a couple of clippings of huge multimillion dollar punitive damage awards in civil cases, and send along a photocopy of a news report showing a plaintiff being awarded a few million dollars. That's enough to give any Bad Guy second thoughts!

Q. By my personal observation, the great Good Guy successes in business take at least five years to show encouraging profit. Aside from patience and frugality, most had funding . . . venture capital, business loans, other backing. How does a Good Guy seek such help?

A. I disagree with your timetable! Regardless of size, any business generating a good product or service for its clients will begin to show signs of support, revenue, and even profit by the end of a full year. Suppliers and financial resources are quick to recognize Good Guys who pay their bills, keep their promises, work with great energy and need financial input and support for greater growth. It is a cop-out when a floundering entrepreneur claims that all he needs to become a great success is a sudden infusion of dollar support.

When the positive signs are there, the lenders, investors, and supportive bankers will not be hard to find.

Q. Describe a typical Good Guy sales "close." Is it similar to, in sales parlance, "the assumptive close?"

A. I have two answers for this. The first is the philosophy practiced by the scores of salespersons my own company employed. Ask a lot of questions, respond with information and assistance, diplomatically introduce the benefits and values of your product or service, and from time to time expose a buying opportunity, supported by special benefits, with a deadline. They practiced a normal "close" because they had to ask for the order sooner or later.

My own procedure was never to give a business prospect a single opportunity to say "no." Sooner or later, the prospect will become impatient to do business with our firm. This attitude drove my salespeople crazy, and they were probably right! So maybe an ideal organization has both cultivators and harvesters!

Q. Many successful people are approached by friends or relatives seeking to borrow money to start a new enterprise. What's your advice on this?

A. Become very businesslike. Conduct the conversation in an office, never in a residence. Take notes carefully. Ask many questions. Examine the business plan carefully. Ask about the borrower's experience in the field involved. Make certain that the borrower is investing some personal funds, so that he or she will be a loser in the event of failure, not just gambling your funds. Insist that the transaction be a formal loan, with written terms, dates of repayment, details, etc. Finally, watch for these danger signs: Entrepreneur has inadequate experience in that field; failed in the last job but has plenty of good excuses; moved recently from one residence to another, thereby adding a second source of stress to the speculative business plans; has many active outside interests and lacks the single-minded obsession to carry a new enterprise to success.

Q. How can you be so certain that Nice Guys finish first, when there are so many apparently successful Bad Guys making lots of money and enjoying a good life?

A. Many are there temporarily, and eventually drift downhill. Others lead angry and belligerent lives, and are doomed to short-lived success. Certainly, some in our free society defy the odds and stay on top despite constant conniving and conspiracy. But talent and professionalism, combined with the attitude of living "on the give," are the more certain paths to wealth and lifelong satisfaction.

Q. A Good Guy must withstand impatience from his family, perhaps early comparisons to more successful relatives or others, etc. How do you keep the Good Guy attitude in slow early times, when surrounded by this type of atmosphere?

A. Be prepared to live frugally! I came from a family of limited means, well prepared for such a life. I was fortunate to meet and marry a marvelous young woman from a poor background, who never expected or demanded anything beyond our means. With this situation at home, all outside pressures were meaningless. By the way, we married 32 days after we met, and believe that it has worked out, since that happened 45 years ago.

Q. In your Preface, you refer to scores of talented and energetic "early dropouts" for every one who makes it to the top of the heap. Where do you see them going wrong?

A. • They get on the wrong ladder in their first jobs. They looked for the highest opening salary instead of opportunity, training, company reputation, advancement potential, etc.

• They are unwilling to sacrifice. The ladder to the top often requires business travel, overtime hours, emergency availability, other personal inconvenience. Owners and managers have made these sacrifices, and promote and favor those with the same qualities.

• They stop learning after the first signs of success. Life's big winners never stop sharpening and broadening their skills.

• They let greed overcome ethics, not realizing how quickly they pass the point of no return. In most cases, eventually, Bad Guys Finish Last, Nice Guys Finish First!

Q. In Chapter 3 on developing employees, you offer an anecdote on erosion of authority caused by an exceptional
performer who feels entitled to break the rules of the workplace. This is a very common problem. How should Good
Guys deal with it?

A. One confrontation at the most carefully selected moment
usually works. Wait patiently for the perpetrator to behave
so outrageously that his or her actions are indefensible.

   Meet in the presence of a third party (as a witness and
for extra impact). Review how valuable the employee is to
the business, but also how and why your right to enforce
workplace rules is even more important.

   Listen to his explanation, and give him a face-saving
"out."

   Conclude forcefully, but without anger, that he has "used
up his lifetime quota" of usurping your authority in the
workplace. He'll get the message!

   If the action is repeated, he must be dismissed regardless
of the consequences.

Q. In Chapter 5, you sound negative about hiring relatives for
positions in a family business. Why?

A. Definitely not so! Sons, daughters and other relatives are a
great source of continuity, loyalty, experience and a positive
image to the public.

   I do warn about these dangers: expectations so high on
both sides that neither party has a convenient escape hatch;
premature and excessive executive income and benefits for
the relatively new recruit; and the absence of a clear written
agreement on what was promised and what was *not*
promised!

CHAPTER 16

◇

How Good Guys Share Their Bounty— Often Receiving Unexpected Rewards

Life "On the Give" to Community and Profession Brings Satisfaction and Surprising By-Products

Many of the happiest, most respected and prosperous professionals and executives I have met are those who are personally "on the give" to worthy causes in their community, industry and circles of interest. In both money and voluntary time, they extend to others the same opportunity and education that have enriched their own lives.

They give freely and generously without expecting repayment, but the rewards come anyway. The world indeed is a huge balance scale, measuring and repaying the contributions of each individual. The more you give, the more this magic system repays you.

Generous givers enjoy recognition and good will. They find unexpected and pleasing contacts with high-level VIPs they never knew. They enjoy mental health that is well above average. As a matter of fact, we have never met a neurotic philanthropist.

The best places to invest your extended life "on the give" are your local community, or in a business or professional trade association. They need people and "doers." In fact, the count of those who give money is larger than the count of those who give time and creativity. Your time in person is needed even more than your checkbook.

Here are some practical ideas on getting started.

1. Put aside an additional sum of money to be given to good causes. Give often, as you hear of "milestones" in the lives of clients, colleagues, suppliers, and others whom you both respect and need in your business.

You'll find plenty of opportunities to make a voluntary gift on the occasion of any milestone. Examples are a birth, graduation, wedding, anniversary, corporate expansion, election or promotion of an individual to an important civic or corporate function, honorary banquet, fund-raising event, and so forth. Occasions for celebration are countless.

Even when you are not solicited, find a cause important to the individual involved, and send a voluntary gift in his or her honor. The individual will be notified and will remember!

2. Try to start teaching . . . something . . . somewhere! Students learn and grow up in an academic world, taught by professional teachers who spend lives in the classroom.

A guest lecturer, an adjunct professor, or a voice of experience from the business world outside is most welcome and informative. There are many such opportunities.

Milt began doing this several decades ago, when his business was small and the demands on his time were many, and there was an element of sacrifice. But the gratification, the countless students touched, and the unexpected recognition from community and industry alike, have been beyond expectation. By giving, he was planting seeds, after which the world's "magic balance scale" went to work.

3. Pick one special cause in which to get more deeply involved. It may be an industry committee, a civic club, an educational institution, a political movement, or some specialized organization pursuing its own agenda to make the world better.

Your mental health will strengthen, several of those you meet may become long-term partners in other positive enterprises, and your own business organization will benefit as a wider circle of admirers appreciate you as a "giver."

4. Offer and give prizes and awards, and sponsor events at conventions in your own profession or industry.

I know several executives who, lacking the confidence to make major speeches, distribute prizes and awards to tennis or golf winners or other achievers at outings or conventions. They are made happy by participating, they have a few moments in the spotlight and they enjoy the dual benefits of being on the give as well as benefitting from that same magic balance scale.

Have you heard the popular expression: "Give till it hurts!"? My answer for the Good Guys of the world: "It *never* hurts!"

Finally, we both recommend that every socially conscious or community conscious executive consider joining the Business for Social Responsibility (BSR), 1030 15th Street N.W., Suite 1010, Washington, DC 20005.

BSR has grown from 50 founders to a national business association with more than 800 member companies, a board of directors comprised of distinguished leaders from the private sector, and a series of program initiatives for businesses needing such advice. Membership includes some of America's most innovative and respected companies such as AT&T, Ben & Jerry's, Body Shop USA, Church & Dwight, Coopers & Lybrand, Federal Express, Fel-Pro, the Gap, Hallmark Cards, Home Depot, Honeywell, Levi Strauss, Lotus Development, Polaroid, Quad/Graphics, Reebok, Silicon Graphics, Stride Rite, Taco Bell, Time Warner and Viacom.

BSR can give you business-to-business information on "best practices," practical business tools, educational seminars, research publications and specific meetings on issues of corporate social responsibility. You can also get a copy of BSR's membership directory, which is updated annually. In a dozen locations nationwide, BSR also supports networks that coordinate the delivery of local programs and services.

If you need a membership application and schedule of dues, or have any questions, call the San Francisco office at 415-865-2500. Robert H. Dunn was president and CEO at the time this book was written.

Membership dues supply only about 1/3 of the funds needed by this organization to function. The rest comes from voluntary contributions and grants. Membership dues range from $150 a year for companies with annual revenue below $100,000 to $15,000 a year for companies with annual revenues over $5 billion.

Five True-Life Stories from the Diaries of "Givers" Show That Unexpected Rewards Follow Trail of Good Guys!

Generous Decision Followed by Wedding

Evelyn M., a recent widow, received an invitation to an annual event she and her late husband had always attended. It was a two-day conference at a nearby college campus, and the sponsor organization also was soliciting annual pledges to help fund its scholarship activities. Evelyn was emotionally unprepared to attend, and, while financially secure, she no longer enjoyed the executive income her husband had generated. She called her daughter, Barbara, who had a professional position in a nearby city.

Barbara's response was immediate: "This organization was very important to Dad, and he was always generous to it. I would like to attend to keep our family involved, and I will give a personal gift in honor of Dad's memory."

Barbara was 35, and so completely involved in her successful career that she had neglected her social life and thoughts of a family. However, during one of the panel discussions at the gathering, she met Howard, an attorney, age 39, shy and not socially aggressive, who was attending the event for the first time in behalf of *his* ailing parents.

After the meeting, Barbara and Howard had lunch together and discovered they had a great deal in common. A wedding followed within a year. This was six years ago.

The happy household now has two small children, plus two parents who were introduced early, by their own family experiences, into the joy of doing and giving in behalf of others. I suspect and hope that their two young children are destined to grow up to enjoy a productive and rewarding life "on the give."

Declined Revenue Generates Greater Reward for Milt

I received an advertising contract for two pages in consecutive monthly issues from a Midwest wholesaler who had never advertised in the magazine before. A page costs several thousand dollars, and I called the wholesaler out of curiosity. Here's the conversation:

Milt: "Joe, I noticed this ad contract, and we thank you very much. What's this all about?"

Joe: "We have a brand-new 200-page catalog, and two new lines. We love your magazine and thought that would be a good place to tell the world about it."

M: "Joe, thanks; we appreciate your confidence. I know you're aware that full-page ads are very costly, but more important, you are paying for national circulation, and your own trade area covers less than 10 percent of that. Have you thought about all that 90 percent waste?"

J: "Milt, my partner felt the same way, but we had to get the word out. Our own mailing list is in terrible shape, and we know that everybody reads your magazine."

M: "Joe, I have another idea. Send me a catalog, and we will review it briefly in our "Catalog Review" section in the back of the magazine. There's no charge for this. Also, I will check my mailing list in the several states you serve, and arrange for you to make a mailing, offering the catalog, to all of our subscribers in those states. Your mailing and handling costs will be a fraction of what you intended to spend on the ad. Then if that doesn't work, you can reconsider running those very expensive ads in the magazine."

J: "Milt, if you say so, we'll give it a try. And my partner is going to love you when I tell him you saved us a few thousand bucks!"

The mailing proceeded. The wholesaler got exceptional requests for the catalog, and quickly opened several new accounts with retailers he had not known previously. The plans for the expensive ads were scrapped.

A few months later, I met Joe personally at a trade convention. He mentioned the entire incident thankfully, and asked me: "Milt, how can you stay in business by turning down advertising revenue?" My answer was simple and truthful: "Joe, I have learned that you can't go wrong doing the right thing!"

On the next day of the convention, Joe was back to me with another question: "Milt, here is a list of my 14 most important suppliers whose brands I wholesale. Look it over, and tell me how many of them are your advertisers."

I looked at the list, and identified four advertisers and ten nonadvertisers.

Joe said to me: "Milt, you have a great magazine, and those other ten guys ought to be in there, too! Maybe they don't listen to your advertising representatives, but they sure will listen to me, because I handle a lot of their goods. Do you mind if I contact them?"

I gave Joe the green light, but asked him not to put on too much pressure. The following year, we had ad contracts from four of the ten "holdouts" on the list. The revenue generated from these national advertisers was a large multiple of what had first been offered to us by the wholesaler himself.

The moral of this story is for the Good Guys of the world: You can't go wrong doing the right thing!

Volunteer Community Teacher
Becomes Corporate VIP

William J., an attorney employed "in-house" on the staff of an insurance company, enjoyed teaching in his community as part of a program called "Community Talent." He periodically lectured to high school juniors and seniors on various legal matters. His professional joy and enthusiasm spilled over to students as he discussed career options, interesting legal cases, how civil and criminal courts work, questions adults should ask before selecting a lawyer, the will and estate options of their parents and grandparents, and other matters the average public school student would never hear professionally in the classroom.

The students looked forward eagerly to William's periodic appearances, particularly when he began to give his students "legal puzzles" at the outset of the class, and then discussed the alternative solutions.

One of his students, Janice, was so impressed by William and his personal enthusiasm that she bragged about him to her parents and told them that she was considering a law career. Janice's father, an entrepreneur and top corporate executive, decided to attend one class. He obtained permission, and sat in to see for himself. Afterward, he approached William with an unexpected job offer:

"Mr. Jones, our corporation needs someone like you! Not only do we have an opening for a corporate attorney, but even more important, we have a couple of dozen middle-level executives who would benefit tremendously from the very type of knowledge you are able to communicate so effectively.

"I'd like you to consider joining our company as a corporate attorney, officer, prospective member of the board, and most important, with the added responsibility of giving executive seminars a few times a year. I think it's vital for each of our middle-level executives to know more about how criminal and civil courts work, how to avoid legal entanglements, the do's and don'ts of their corporate behavior, and your answers to their many questions on these subjects. In fact, I wouldn't mind attending every one of those lectures myself!"

This exceptional opportunity, in both status and earnings potential, was too great for William to resist. He spent his career doing the things he enjoyed most, with title and status beyond what he had anticipated in life, but also with the assurance that he would never give up the time devoted to "Community Talent."

Gralla Acquires, Rebuilds Troubled Magazine After Fast, Unique "Character Investigation"

I was in the office of an attorney, Mr. J, the family friend of a trade magazine publisher who had died suddenly. Mr. J's job was to settle the estate. I explained that we wished to make an immediate purchase of one of the late publisher's magazines.

I explained further that we were a relatively small and unknown publishing firm, but that we had been researching the possibility of a magazine launch in the same field. The late publisher's magazine was running dead last in a field of three. We could save six months by an immediate acquisition instead of a new launch. We were willing to pay a decent price for that opportunity, even though the existing magazine was showing no profit. Here is a condensed summary of the subsequent conversation:

J: "Mr. Gralla, I have many other matters of priority. We have real estate, a portfolio of securities, inheritance taxes, and other matters with higher dollar values. The magazine is just a very small part of the estate. Come back and see me in three months."

G: "Mr. J, this magazine has weak circulation and staff, and is barely hanging on. If you lose just a few advertisers after the publisher's death, there will be nothing left. Put another way, if you wait three months, you will have nothing to sell!"

J: "How can I trust what you have to say? How can I advise the widow?"

G: "I can't answer that except to say I know this field, I am here now, and I want to offer you a quick transaction at a very fair price."

J: "I don't know you at all, and I have no time to research this field. Would you be willing to let me investigate you personally and immediately, so that I can trust your words and actions, and so advise the widow?"

G: "Absolutely . . . that's a great idea!"

Mr. J then called in his secretary, and she took notes while he asked me briefly about the community where I live, the people who knew me in that community, and a variety of printers, bankers, brokers, suppliers, and others with whom Gralla Publications and I did business. I gave him the names of my town mayor, synagogue rabbi, school board members, printer, stockbroker, etc. He took all the names, and started this unusual investigation.

Within 48 hours, Mr. J called my brother and partner Larry, and quickly concluded prompt and fair acquisition of the magazine by Gralla Publications. The magazine was revitalized almost overnight by some of our best staff people, and became one of the largest and most successful in our company, leading us into the publishing "major leagues." The widow and the estate received a quick and fair cash settlement for a magazine that certainly would have disappeared if neglected for a few months. In fact, Larry threw in a bonus to the seller based on the magazine's growth for the first few years, and the seller thereby received a generous additional reward.

The lawyer later sent me a beautiful "thank-you" letter summarizing the entire sequence of events, and I treasure this as much as the fortune generated by the magazine! He also later confessed to me that he aborted his unusual investigation after the third phone call. He was convinced he was dealing with a trustworthy Good Guy!

Courageous Decision on Charitable Gift
Leads to Multiple Business Accounts

Computer supply salesman Danny Blackman, 29, faced a very tough personal decision.

Despite his moderate income, Danny had been fulfilling his family tradition of giving some of his income to charitable and community causes. He also had been allocating some of his giving to causes favored by business clients. He made these small gifts whenever he heard of a milestone in the life of a client—a birth, wedding, graduation, death of a parent, for example. The gifts usually went to an announced charitable cause—a school, hospital, etc., in honor of the family.

One day, Danny read of the death of an elderly parent of an important corporate executive. The charity listed in the obituary did not meet his standards. In the interest of being diplomatic, he wrote this letter:

Dear Mr. Smith:

I would like to make a gift in honor of the memory of your beloved mother. Do you have another cause in addition to the one listed in the newspaper?

Sincerely,

Danny Blackman.

The next day Smith called Blackman. Here's a summary of the conversation.

Smith: "Mr. Blackman, this is Gardner Smith. Thanks for your thoughtful generosity about my mother's memory. Is there anything wrong with (Charity X) mentioned in the obituary?"

Blackman: "Mr. Smith, it's gracious of you to call. You can call me Danny. I don't have a lot to give, and I'd rather favor another cause."

S: "Danny, level with me. I won't hold it against you."

B: "Okay . . . it's just that (Charity X) hasn't met some of the NCIB standards for a couple of years, and didn't report at all last year."

S: "What's the NCIB?"

B: "The National Charities Information Bureau. It gathers data on lots of known and lesser-known charities. It sends reports, on request, to people like you and me. My family has subscribed to NCIB for years."

S: "That's very interesting. With all the solicitations I get, I wish I had known about NCIB. Can you send me the report?"

B: "I'll go one better. I'll send the report, and I'll also send NCIB a gift and ask them to put you on the mailing list for a year."

S: "Thanks, Danny . . . and send me your business card while you're at it."

A week later, Smith called Danny again.

S: "Danny, this is Gardner Smith. Thanks for the very helpful NCIB report on (Charity X). On another subject, Smith Enterprises has a new operations manager who's reviewing our entire computer functions. I want an honest kid like you looking over his shoulder."

B: "Thanks for the confidence, Mr. Smith. I'm not sure I have all the answers. May I bring one of our technical experts?"

S: "Danny, as long as you're there, I'm in good hands."

The story does not end after Smith quickly became a major client for computer hardware, software, and related services supplied by Danny's employer. Smith was so impressed by Blackman's honesty, guts and tradition of charity that he often bragged about Danny to his country club friends. He gave out Danny's cards, and reminded his golfing buddies about the NCIB as well. For all his business life, Danny never lacked trusting clients!

My moral from this true story: You never go wrong doing the right thing!

---- ◇ ----

GOOD GUYISM APPLIED: ENJOY THE "BEST OF THE BEST" WITH ADRIANE

The word "philanthropist" (from the Greek, lover of one's fellow man) conjures up many images. Oddly enough, a number of them are not flattering . . . women who give just to be seen at society charity balls, men who give publicly and act like devils privately, special privileges in education and health care for those wealthy enough to give an endowment, and, of course, tax angles. . . .

It would be ingenuous to say that I've never observed such things in the upper echelons of giving. But, despite what you might think, I haven't seen it much. For most wealthy people, particularly those who made their own way, giving is "old hat." In many instances, they gave money and time when they had very little of either. Young entrepreneurs, who played ball in the evenings with underprivileged kids, eventually prosper and give thousands to fresh air funds. The best checks I write are to the Forgotten Children's Fund in Seattle and the Valerie Fund, for kids with cancer, in New Jersey.

If I could give you one Good Guy rule it would be this: Find the time to *give* your time for one half hour every week.

And now the concluding observation: I have found there is something almost mystical in giving. For certain, there is a whole body of religious thought led by Christian mystic Catherine

Ponder that postulates a bountiful world and asserts that you get back as you give. Norman Vincent Peale preached it. One charity I know asks for written pledges and then suggests that you fulfill them when extra money comes in. Donors tell me that the money does come in, from some unexpected sources, all the time.

I wonder. What do *you* think?

What I am sure of is that good people give. Good people are often rich in wealth, information and promise. Therefore, giving brings you together with the best of the best. So, good things are likely to happen to you, on the inside as well as on the outside.

I'll go further. If you have been looking for a new road, and you picked up this book as your success manual, I suggest that you set aside your immediate personal goals for a moment. Make the very first act on your new road to sure success an act of charity. In the midst of your cluttered desk and busy schedule find the phone book, with the number of the nearest soup kitchen, literacy center or hospital volunteer program.

Bibliography

Abraham, Jay. *Money-Making Secrets of Marketing Genius Jay Abraham*. Rolling Hill Estates, Calif.: Abraham Publishing Group, 1994.

Allen, Kathleen R. *Launching New Ventures*. Chicago: Upstart Publishing Co., 1995.

Deep, Sam, and Lyle Sussman. *What to Ask When You Don't Know What to Say*. Englewood Cliffs, N.J.: Prentice Hall, 1993.

DeVos, Rich. *Compassionate Capitalism*. New York: Penguin-Plume, 1993.

Friedman, Nancy J. *Telephone Skills from A to Z*. Menlo Park, Calif.: Crisp Publications, 1995.

Hanan, Mack, and Peter Karp. *Competing on Value*. New York: Amacom, 1991.

Jandt, Fred E. *Win-Win Negotiating*. New York: Wiley, 1985.

Kennedy, Daniel S. *The Ultimate Sales Letter*. Holbrook, Mass.: Bob Adams, Inc., 1990.

Mullen, James X. *The Simplest Art of Greatness.* New York: Viking, 1995.

National Charities Information Bureau, 19 Union Square West, New York, NY 10003.

Rosenblatt, Nate. *Money Making Sales Letters.* Round Lake, Conn.: Round Lake Publishing, 1990.

White, Kate. *Why Good Girls Don't Get Ahead but Gutsy Girls Do.* New York: Warner Books, 1995.

Wilson, Jerry R. *Word-of-Mouth Marketing.* New York: Wiley, 1994.

Index

About the Authors

Milt's Parallel Business Lifetimes
Were Sources for This Book

The rich experiences of Milton Gralla's two concurrent business lifetimes have contributed to this practical guide to financial success and personal achievement.

As editorial director of 20-plus national business and trade magazines, in such diverse fields as construction, manufacturing, real estate, travel, banking, design and retailing, he enjoyed a matchless view of American business life. Over decades, he watched the winners and losers, Good Guys and Bad Guys, leaders and followers, staid corporate executives and dreaming entrepreneurs. His magazines chronicled their strategies and results.

As co-founder of a two-man, one-room, one-magazine "publishing company," Milton (with his brother Larry) nurtured Gralla Publications into a publishing and trade show empire that was sold (in 1983) for $73 million. As his own enterprise became a laboratory for the skills and methods described in this book, he learned by making many of the mistakes described in these pages, but never lost faith in the philosophy that Good Guys do, indeed, finish first.

Milton also is a popular lecturer, seminar leader, and college teacher of the business methods and philosophy now assembled here in book form for the first time. In private life, he's a bridge fiend, a tennis bum, and an educational philanthropist, with residences in New Jersey and Florida.

Adriane Finds That Credentials
and Hard Work Are Not Enough—
The Good Guy System Brings Success

Every time Adriane G. Berg is introduced at one of her seminars, her credentials are given differently. Editor of *Wealth-*

builder, the financial newsletter; attorney; chairperson of the New York Bar Association; author of 18 books on personal finance; speaker; radio and television talk show host; journalist. And her favorite title: mother of Arthur and Rosie.

But, that's just for the present. Adriane also has been a stockbroker and insurance agent. While she has always had personal success, true and continuous financial success did not come until she applied the Good Guy principles found in this book with consistency and dedication.

Adriane has vast insight into the traits of super-successful people. She meets them as law clients, as fellow members of charity boards, and at international investor conferences.

She is a speaker for dozens of business organizations and chambers of commerce. Adriane has been a top sales producer in the media and insurance industry. Her broadcasts have been sponsored by some of the wealthiest and most powerful entrepreneurs in America.

In her many pursuits, Adriane has seen the business world from the point of view of the struggling novice, the world-weary middle manager and the overwhelming and often envied megasuccess.

Her conclusion is clear. The principles espoused in the Good Guy method work, and they may be the only methods that work with consistency to assure financial success in business.